Feeling
Dressage

Feeling
Dressage

By Ruth Sabine Schaefer

Foreword by Conrad Schumacher

ECLIPSE PRESS

Lexington, Kentucky

Library of Congress Control Number:
2002114037

ISBN 1-58150-093-9

Printed in The United States
First Edition: April 2003

Distributed to the trade by
National Book Network
4720-A Boston Way
Lanham, MD 20706
1.800.462.6420

a division of
Blood-Horse Publications
PUBLISHERS SINCE 1916

CONTENTS

Foreword 7

1   Dressage: A Foundation 9

2   Physical and Mental Abilities of the Horse 11

3   Preparation for the Rider 23

4   The Rider's Seat..................................29

5   Gaits and How to Ride Them 49

6   The Aids 63

7   How to Structure a Riding Session 83

8   Training the Green Horse/The Scale of Training 99

9   In the Arena 119

10 Movements 129

11 Dressage Terms 175

Appendix — Equipment for the Horse 189

About the Author 202

Foreword

In the quest to master the techniques of classical dressage, riders sometimes forget an equally important component of successful riding — achieving the feel. As I travel around the world training riders, the biggest hurdle I see them face — whatever their age or experience level — is feel.

To succeed at dressage, rider and horse must have talent, commitment, discipline, and a training foundation based on the principles of classical dressage. At the top ranks of the sport you will find riders and horses who received a very intense basic foundation.

To ride good dressage, the rider must know all the aids, possible reactions of the horse, its reasons for reacting, and all movements. This means a rider needs to learn all techniques and essential knowledge. Equally important, the rider must learn to understand what he or she is feeling and how each movement *should* feel when performed correctly.

I am often asked to suggest literature to help the beginning to intermediate rider understand how to develop feeling from technique. Ruth Schaefer's book describes in a systematic way how to achieve the right feeling. Her concepts make this book unique and especially valuable for riders who often train by themselves.

Learning feel for the horse and for the moment in the rider's own body takes a lifelong commitment. Commitment implies continuous self-awareness and analysis of the horse's reactions to develop technique into the real goal — the art of feeling.

Feeling Dressage underlines that we must never forget the importance of dressage work to any horse. It is important that we understand dressage is the way of gymnasticising the horse.

Schaefer stresses that dressage applies to all horse types and is the necessary foundation of every riding discipline. This makes the book appealing not only to the dressage enthusiast but to any rider who understands "gymnasticising" riding as an important part of a horse's training. A horse must be supple and obedient to perform well in any discipline.

The detailed yet easy-to-understand descriptions help the rider comprehend and visualize his or her goal and how certain movements should feel. The definitions and analogies draw a very clear picture and assist the rider in translating theory into practice.

There are plenty of books that list all the rider's aids and all the movements in sequence. Usually they do just that — list them. *Feeling Dressage* gives the learning rider tools to comprehend how to use aids, feel their influence, read the horse's reactions, and know the steps in which to teach a new movement to the horse.

Conrad Schumacher

1 | Dressage: A Foundation

We want to take care and not vex the horse and spoil its friendly grace, which like the fragrance of a flower, once vanished will never return.

Antoine de la Baume Pluvinel

We sometimes learn to do things a specific way without knowing why. Riding is like that. Your teacher will instruct you to use your aids in a certain manner to bring the horse on the bit or perform a movement. You often do it without asking or thinking because it has always been done this way in dressage. Your trainer is successful and well known, so it must be right. Most of the time it is.

But it often helps to know why we ride classical dressage as we do. Many people who reject dressage riding would be more open to it if they first knew the whys. This does not mean that it is the only way to train a horse. Different goals require different training systems. Often one system is promoted as the only way or the best way to train horses and riders, but various methods are related in lots of ways. They have to be because we work with the same subject: the horse.

For example, several movements in dressage are similar to Western riding. The dressage pirouette in walk or canter basically shows the same kind of movement as the rollback or spinning in Western riding. All these turn the horse's forehand around the hind legs. Both riding styles emphasize a stop achieved with only soft use of the rein aids. The hind legs initiate the transition instead of the horse putting all his weight on the front legs. Lateral movements, circles, and serpentines to flex and supple the horse are used. Both disciplines use flexion, impulsion, and collection, only trained with different aids for different purposes.

Keep in mind that dressage work also looks different on different horses. High knee action and a very high-set neck make Friesians, Lippizans, and Andalusians ideal-looking dressage horses. They are bred with the ability for the highest levels of dressage and present a different picture doing dressage.

While dressage at the highest levels is its own riding style, basic dressage training can apply to all riding disciplines. It is a general training of the horse based on gymnastic exercises that enable the horse to use his body in a comfortable, effective way to fulfill the rider's wishes. Whether you ride trail or endurance horses, jumpers, Western or gaited horses, a fundamental understanding of dressage makes it possible to handle any horse safely and easily.

Dressage develops the horse physically and mentally and enables him to perform movements and paces based on his natural abilities. A horse trained in dressage becomes obedient, powerful, and comfortable for the rider. The rider gains an elastic, balanced seat, precise coordination of the aids, and control of his own body so completely that the rider-horse partnership happens with harmony and ease. The horse should obey us, but this should happen in a partnership and not with the rider forcing the horse to perform in ways that are uncomfortable or painful.

This willingness to follow the rider's aids while being supple, obedient, and without resistance or hesitation is known as submissiveness, or *Durchlaessigkeit*. It is the cornerstone of dressage at every level.

Classical dressage requires mastery, though, of more than theory. The educated rider who *feels* dressage brings out its true beauty. In this book, I present some of the basics of dressage for the beginning and intermediate rider while also explaining how gaits and movements should feel.

2 | Physical and Mental Abilities of the Horse

A chieving success with a horse will depend upon your understanding of his instinctive nature, as well as familiarity with his physical and mental capabilities. We do assume a standard training sequence for the majority of horses. But when we work with a horse, we must always adjust the training sequences to his special needs.

The horse's behavior is mainly based on survival instincts. To understand, handle, and ride horses, we need to understand that they perceive their environment completely differently than we do. They feel and observe many things we do not even register. Recognizing and meeting the horse's instinctual needs will greatly influence how well and quickly he learns.

Herd and flight instinct

Wild horses live in groups and move almost continuously. So it is important that we allow the horse enough space to move around, fresh air, and company. Every horse, however, must be slowly trained to be comfortable occasionally going without the company of other horses.

Sudden noises and unfamiliar objects stimulate the horse's flight instinct. Depending on the distance to the noise or object, a horse will either express curiosity or protect himself by running away. Fleeing instinctively often happens in a state of panic. Because a horse's perception is so different from ours, he may perceive something as threatening that we haven't even noticed. Only when he is attacked directly or when there is no escape will a horse counterattack to defend himself.

Ranking order

Within every group of horses is a strict social structure. The strong, smart, brave, or experienced will rank higher than those horses that exhibit fewer leadership qualities. Constant quarrels about rank are part of the horse's life and are instinctive. A herd of wild horses could not survive without this strict social structure.

The leaders of a horse herd are the main stallion and the lead mare. The dominant members of a herd supply the group with security against enemies, participate in educating the younger ones, lead to grazing and water, take the risks, and often shelter an inferior from the attacks of other group members. Horses of minor rank respect and obey the leader and get safety in return. Whether it is food, water, or shelter, the superiors are first. The superior members must re-establish their dominance from time to time, as the inferior horses will try to move higher in rank.

The relationship between horse and human is also ruled by this ranking order. The human must have the dominant position. Being the superior does not mean that we must establish this position with physical force. Consistent and smart behavior along with a punishment/reward combination does the job. Horses are able immediately to judge the rank of other humans as well as horses. Because the horse is stronger and heavier than we are, dominance is essential for a safe, functioning relationship and progress in education.

You will observe some horse people constantly hitting and yelling at their horses. This is mostly a sign of their own fear, insecurity, and lack of knowledge about how to communicate with horses. Hitting and yelling will produce either a terrified or dangerous horse because sooner or later the horse may fight back.

To be the dominant partner in the relationship with a horse involves more than being superior and commanding. As the horse's leader, we have the great responsibility to care for him and treat him fairly in all situations. The horse instinctively relies on this and respects and trusts you as he would the dominant horse in a herd. We need to evaluate what we can ask of the horse at certain stages of training without demanding more than the horse is capable of doing at that particular point.

The horse's senses

We also have to keep in mind that the horse's hearing and sense of smell are far more developed than ours. Although his vision is poorly developed by our standards, horses have a visual field of almost 360 degrees and can see far better in darkness than we do. These perception differences can cause us to misinterpret the horse's behavior.

How do horses learn?

The horse is an animal of habit that learns through conditioning. A horse always correlates cause and consequence. Repetition and immediate reaction to a certain behavior are necessary. This means reward or punishment must follow behavior immediately. Otherwise the horse cannot make the connection.

A note about punishment

Punishing rarely means hitting. Outwitting the horse or making his misbehavior uncomfortable is much more effective. Never try to break a horse's spirit. You will destroy his personality. Do not punish a horse when he is afraid, does not understand something, or has just learned something new.

Finding the right approach to correct undesirable behavior is very important. For example, when a horse shies, one possible reaction is to punish the horse severely. This, however, will cause the horse to shy again at the same occasion because he fears the memory of the punishment, not the actual cause of his fright.

The opposite reaction is to fuss and calm the horse excessively. Riders often do this when they feel afraid themselves. Again, the horse will continue to shy when exposed to the same situation because he will have been convinced his fear was legitimate.

Finding the right approach is important to overcome the shying. Apply your aids both rigorously and reassuringly at the same time. The horse should sense that you are determined but also protective and patient. Here you have to play the role of the leader, with all its responsibilities.

One good way to deal with a horse shying is delaying the approach to the scary object or spot. Pass the fearful object with enough distance that the horse may still observe it but keeps moving. Gradually get closer to the object by a few feet each time. The horse has time to get used to it and time to forget about past associations. You also can ride the horse in a shoulder-in or leg-yield position passing the object, always facing the horse's head away from the fright. It often is helpful not to show the fearful spot directly to the horse after it initially spooked. Some horses fear the object the more we show it to them. Still, you want to let some horses explore the situation in their own time.

Mental abilities

On top of his instinctive nature, each horse has his own temperament, character, ability to concentrate, depth of memory, degree of willingness, and capacity to adapt. All of these characteristics are hereditary, although we can improve or spoil them through conditioning and education. Negative inherited qualities can be corrected only partially or temporarily. Patient observation of the horse is necessary to judge his behavior. The education process should always let the horse keep his individuality. A relationship in the form of a partnership should be the goal, with trust and obedience as the basis.

We have to adjust and structure our training and handling to existing conditions. So we treat a nervous and easily frightened horse calmly and patiently. The resentful horse needs a purposeful rider who can encourage the horse to be willing and happy in work. A lazy horse needs a strong rider who can make the horse try harder, whereas the extremely sensitive horse needs a very quiet and tactful rider who sits very smoothly.

Mentally strong horses have strong personalities. Usually they are extremely intelligent and secure but often very stubborn, showing resistance easily. But when an experienced rider is able to overcome this and create a partnership, these horses are capable of performance at the highest levels. For a less experienced rider, a less intelligent horse with not so much ego would be the better choice.

PHYSICAL ABILITIES

Correct physical conformation dictates the quality of a dressage horse. Besides, the horse gains much when he makes a good overall impression. But beauty is not necessary for dressage success. Correct training, in fact, can mold an average-looking horse into one that moves beautifully.

There is no horse without fault in conformation. What we have to do is distinguish the important from the unimportant, and learn to get along with minor faults. In addition, the horse's overall suitability depends not solely on good conformation but on mental abilities as well. A perfectly built horse cannot achieve top performance if he lacks temperament, character, or ridability. A horse with some conformation faults but wonderful mental qualities may develop into a brilliant performer.

To succeed at dressage, a horse needs good conformation.

How the horse's muscles reveal if he is trained correctly

Physically correct, supple, and regularly used muscles get better blood circulation and are therefore nourished better. They will develop new muscle fibers and grow thicker. So we are able to judge a horse's stage of physical training and the correctness of this training by seeing which muscles are well developed.

A horse gets more muscular, stronger, healthier, and more beautiful when trained correctly and sufficiently. Look at the horse's neck. If the horse is ridden correctly and made supple on the bit, his upper neck muscles get stronger. The upper neck grows higher and wider during training and achieves a convex form. The opposite happens with the under side. Used very little, these muscles will be less strong and visible. The opposite of this would be a neck with extremely developed and very evident lower neck muscles and little development of the upper neck muscles. Here we can assume that the training is not correct.

The development of the neck muscles also depends on the horse's gender, age, conformation, and breed. Stallions naturally develop a very big neck because of their hormones. Warmbloods commonly develop more visible neck muscles than Thoroughbreds. A horse that is anatomically flawed with a ewe or stag neck, for example, can be changed only partly and with difficulty.

The back muscles should be developed so that the vertebrae are not higher than the muscles, especially in the croup area. The croup should look round with strong thigh muscles, the flanks not hollow, and the buttocks well developed.

DESIRED CONFORMATION OF A DRESSAGE HORSE

The dressage horse should have long, harmonious body lines and expressive motion in his paces. The hindquarter, being the motor, must be strong enough to carry weight and develop impulsion. The forehand with head and neck must be able to elevate during training.

The head: The head must fit the rest of the horse's body. The horse must be "good through the jowl," meaning the jowl must not be too big and wide. Otherwise the parotid gland (set where the jaw is connected to the neck) gets squeezed when the horse is on the bit.

Insufficient room for the parotid gland combined with a too strongly muscled poll results in a horse that often resents the rein aids, is difficult to flex and get submissive, and has a tendency to keep his head tilted.

The neck: The neck must be sufficiently long, wide at the shoulder, and narrow toward the head. It should come out of the shoulder at an approximately 90-degree angle and not be set too low. The upper neck line is arched upward, slightly longer, and stronger muscled than the lower neck.

Withers: The withers must be sufficiently pronounced and muscled, slightly higher than the croup, and reach far enough into the back.

It is difficult to find a saddle for high and bony withers. Flat and poorly marked withers do not keep the saddle far enough back, and the rider will sit too far up the shoulders, burdening the horse's forehand.

Shoulder: The shoulder must be strongly muscled, long, and sloping. The angle between shoulder and upper forearm should be about 90 degrees. If you imagine a line down to the ground from the horse's shoulder, it will show the length of stride the horse can develop.

A steep shoulder indicates that the horse has not much length of stride in his gaits. A horse with an average slope and length of shoulder still can have good length of stride when the hindquarters are angled well.

Legs: Front and hind legs should be in straight formation. Depending on the incorrectness, poorly formed legs will eventually affect movement and soundness of the horse.

Back: The back must be sufficiently long, with the withers higher than the croup. The distance from the point of shoulder to the last point of the hindquarters should be slightly more than that from the highest point of the withers to the ground. The back should be a little hollow in the middle, well muscled, and show a straight line moving into the croup.

Croup, hindquarters: The croup should be sufficiently long, sloping downward very slightly. The whole hindquarters should be very well muscled around the buttocks. The hip and knee joints should have angles of about 90 degrees.

A croup sloping down too much and differently angled joints will affect movement and impulsion negatively.

UNDESIRED SHAPES

Short, thick neck; strongly developed lower neck muscles: These horses are difficult to ride on the bit. They often have a tense back. Impulsion coming from the hindquarters is restrained. If the neck is sufficiently long and not set too low, much stretching of the horse forward-downward will help to shape the neck.

Long neck: A long neck can balance better than a short one but is also less steady. The horse tends to keep it too short or "rolled in."

Low-set neck: A low-set neck makes collection and elevation of the forehand (see terms in chapter 11) difficult. The horse tends to have too much weight on the forehand.

High-set neck: A high-set neck affects suppleness of the back and the ability to stretch forward-downward. For dressage, a slightly higher set neck is more desirable than a low set.

Ewe neck, "stag" neck: The topline is concave and the lower line is longer, resulting in overdeveloped lower neck muscles and underdeveloped upper neck muscles. Many of these horses have a weakly muscled back because it is kept hollow. They are hard to stretch in the neck. This horse is very difficult to train as the muscle development has to be changed completely.

Swan neck: The swan neck is a long, thin neck, set very high with the upper neck arched too much. The horse is hard to get into a steady head and neck position; he often does not want to connect on the bit and shows evasive movements in the neck. When this horse is brought to an elevated position too early, the "broken neck" may occur (see chapter 11). The horse needs to be ridden in a long and low frame for a long time.

Short back: A short back is usually well muscled and strong, but hard to keep supple. It is, however, more desirable than a long and weak back. Constant relaxing and suppling exercises are necessary to keep it swinging.

Long back: A long back makes it difficult to engage the hind legs sufficiently. Young horses with a long back are not well muscled, so a lot of strengthening is necessary. Generally a long back is very comfortable to sit and easy to keep supple.

Roach back: The roach back is arched upward in the loin area, showing a little bump. These horses tense easily and are hard to get supple and swinging in the back.

Hollow back: The hollow back is weak in the loin area and does not have much power to carry weight. Mostly, these horses are very uncomfortable to sit.

Higher in croup than at withers: Here the forehand is overburdened. It is difficult to keep the saddle in place and to elevate the horse's forehand at a later stage. This conformation can temporarily occur in horses that are still growing. If it stays, the horse is not suitable for competitive dressage. We do not ride such a horse forward-downward for long; the horse is brought into a higher position rather early so it balances better.

Although elegance and beauty are always desirable qualities, a dressage horse does not have to be beautiful. Correct training may bring out his beauty. There are horses that do not inspire a second look when in a stall but become beautiful underneath a good rider.

RIDER AND HORSE — THE RIGHT COMBINATION

Dressage, like all types of riding, is a sport. But unlike most other sports, achieving competitive success in dressage depends on a partnership. To enjoy our sport and achieve our potential, we need to evaluate our own physical and mental capabilities, as well as the capabilities of our partner, the horse. While it is important to consider whether you and your horse work well together, sometimes financial realities dictate that the "right" horse is the one that is affordable. A training program always should be developed to fit the special needs of the rider and the horse, as well as the partnership.

About the rider

One of the great aspects of riding, especially dressage, is that age matters little. You can do it until old age, becoming even more advanced and experienced by the year. Riding with proper technique cannot be achieved in a short time but also doesn't get lost because you get "older." Learning to ride is definitely easier for children, but only a matter of harder work for adults.

Theoretic knowledge is essential for progress. It is even more important when the rider wants to move up the levels. Learn the theory, then experience and feel it with practical riding.

There is an old saying: "Learning to ride means learning self-control." This tells us that one aspect of learning depends on our attitude toward ourselves, the horse, and eventually the trainer. So we need to give ourselves some thought.

Let's assume that you want to achieve more than showing well in front of spectators. You want progress that allows the horse to stay sound and attentive, become physically more beautiful through muscle development, and attain more overall beauty through development of charisma and personality. You want to achieve a partnership, not a predicament, between rider and horse. You want to treat the horse as a partner with an individual character.

To ride dressage, you need to be generally physically fit. You do not have to be extremely strong. What dressage requires is good coordination of the mind and body and a feeling for rhythm and motion.

The theory of the rider's aids is very mechanical, but the successful use of the aids calls for feeling. Learn to develop feeling, which is sensing a certain situation and taking the appropriate action.

Patience, fairness, responsibility, superiority, and discipline are other attributes of the ideal rider.

Never lose your temper. That means self-control. You are the smart and thinking one (that is what we assume), the boss. Earlier we learned about horse behavior and how humans should have higher ranking. But the boss has to be fair. If the rider gets angry and acts unfairly by hitting the horse without any reason, the horse will not understand the action.

Make an honest judgment about your own temperament and nerves. If you are very easily frightened (maybe because you have had a traumatic experience with a horse in the past), choose a rather lazy, calm horse. This gives you a safer feeling as you learn. If you lose patience quickly, do not choose a hot-tempered, skittish partner.

Do not blame your horse for everything. It is mostly your fault. Always be critical about yourself and look for your possible mistakes or incorrect methods. If the learning process stagnates, try alternative ways that may be better for you or your horse. But also find a basic direction in which to move. Switching from one riding technique to the next or trying a new bit or auxiliary rein whenever a problem occurs will not bring the success you want.

About the horse — the ideal schoolmaster

The right horse is important to the learning process. The horse should be willing and calm and have a gentle temperament. More temperamental horses are better suited to experienced riders. The beginner may be frightened and have more difficulty gaining an independent, relaxed seat. However, an easy forward-going, sensitive horse can help a more experienced rider refine his communication by reacting more strongly to his mistakes.

The physical conformation of the horse should ideally match that of his rider: a strongly built horse for a large-framed rider, a smaller horse or pony for a smaller person or child. Ponies are especially good choices for children. They are easier to sit and their physical strength is more in proportion to a child's. Ill-matched partnerships can either overly exert the horse and weaken his soundness or create a dangerous situation for the rider if he is not able to control his horse at all times. This applies especially to children.

The horse should have a solid training foundation. Whether this means first or fourth level is a question of the rider's finances. However, a Grand Prix-trained horse does not make much sense for the beginner. Such horses usually are too sensitive to compensate for the beginner's mistakes. It may not be possible to maintain the horse's training level with a beginning rider until he reaches more advanced stages. There is no point in wasting money.

The horse should walk, trot, and canter in an even and steady pace while remaining relaxed and supple. The canter, especially, must be done easily on both leads and in at least a working pace. Figures and transitions should be done easily, and the horse should go on the bit (for the definition of "on the bit," see chapter 11). The horse must accept the rider's aids and be rather soft to sit. Every more advanced movement the horse knows (for example: lateral movements, turn on the forehand, or turn on the haunches) is great, but not necessary. After solid basic training, the rider will be able to learn new movements together with his horse. This takes longer than learning on an already-trained horse but gives the rider valuable experience.

A widely trained horse that can jump a little and behave reliably on trails in addition to having a basic dressage foundation always is the perfect choice because jumping and trail riding should be part of every beginner's training to achieve overall knowledge and ability.

Every horse ridden by a beginner needs regular schooling, or "retraining," to maintain his intended level. The horse will remain more willing for his rider when worked by the trainer or an advanced rider. This also enables the trainer to teach new movements to the horse and rider simultaneously. The horse then will know and understand faster and better while the learning rider tries the movement but naturally still makes mistakes.

Evaluation of the available horse

Trying to find the above-described ideal horse is very difficult and expensive. If you must choose a less-perfect horse, you should evaluate what the affordable horse offers. This may work as well, especially if a good trainer is on hand to help you and the horse. It may only cost more time.

If your horse has faults or limits due to his conformation, evaluate the limits so you demand only what the horse is able to offer. Many conformational challenges can be overcome to a large degree with specialized training.

Temperamental difficulties and character faults must be considered seriously to develop proper handling.

There are some faults in a horse that are absolutely unsuitable for a beginner: rearing and bucking or a manifested flight instinct that leads the horse to bolt frequently. Besides frightening the rider and therefore obstructing learning, these can threaten the beginner's safety and will definitely take the enjoyment out of the sport.

3 | Preparation for the Rider

Before you actually start riding, learn how to approach and handle a horse. Expand your understanding of riding and training by taking lessons and riding whenever you can. Also read books about horse behavior and training. Take advantage of opportunities to watch other riders — both beginning and advanced. Often it is difficult to see what an advanced rider is doing with his body to influence the horse. Watch the attempts and mistakes of lower-level riders and compare them to your observations of advanced riders.

LUNGEING LESSONS

The most effective method to gain a correct seat as a beginning rider is to take lessons on the lunge line. This is also very valuable for experienced riders who are new to dressage. If you are a secure and advanced rider, you may feel that you can skip this step. However, the dressage seat, especially sitting the gaits, may be a new challenge for you. Lungeing sessions throughout your whole riding career are a helpful addition to successful training. Advanced riders who also have sufficient knowledge about lungeing can do this together — one on the horse, one on the ground. Riding on the lunge line will give you an opportunity to concentrate on your seat without the responsibility of controlling the horse.

Use a reliable, well-trained horse that is easy to sit. For the very first lessons, I advise riding with a saddle or bareback with a vaulting girth to hold onto when needed. The horse should have side reins.

The first lessons should concentrate on giving the rider a feeling for the independent seat, balance, and the influence of body aids. Work with and without stirrups, and practice the dressage seat in all three gaits.

An independent and balanced seat means staying on the horse without holding onto the reins or gripping the horse's sides with your thighs, knees, and calves. The better your ability to sit independently and apply the aids on the lunge line, the better control you will have when you start to ride without the lunge. Your horse will benefit as well — errors made by beginning riders can interfere with a horse's sensitivity and training. Additionally, problems common to beginners or hunter/jumper riders, such as leaning too forward, can develop into bad habits when the rider is too busy managing the horse to achieve the correct seat.

It is far more difficult to overcome bad habits than to learn something new. Do not get frustrated when your trainer has to give the same corrections again and again. Coordinating your whole body takes time. Set goals for yourself and divide them into step-by-step procedures.

One more tip, especially for the adult beginner: try not to use your brain too much at the start. Your mind will understand faster than your body what you are trying to do, but attempting to coordinate the body by thinking too much often creates tension and stiffness. You will use too much muscle to reach your goal. Riding involves the contraction of certain muscles combined with the softening of other muscles. The challenge is to be able to use your feeling as well as your brain to coordinate your body. Here we are again: Feeling! How to interact with a horse, whether from the ground or in the saddle, can be mostly explained in words, but to become a great horse person and rider you need to listen to your body and your intuition.

In the very first exercises, the beginner sits on the horse in the halt. Turn the thighs inward so that the knees lie flat against the saddle. The muscles of the buttocks and inner thighs should not be tense. Let calves and feet relax and hang down, then move the calves back into the right position and into contact with the horse's belly. Feel this contact — don't squeeze, just lean. Stretch your upper body upward; arch your chest so that your upper back vertebrae move forward but the lower ones move back to avoid a hollowed back. Have your instructor move your head, arms, and legs into the right positions.

The next step is to maintain this position in walk and later in trot. During the sitting trot, you will need to hold onto the saddle until you get a feeling for this motion. A great danger in the beginning is to overdo your effort to stay in the correct seat, which will lead to muscle tension. Do short periods of trot work and have walk breaks in between to relax your body before you become tense and bouncing. Try the canter only after you achieve some security in walk and trot. For the first canters hold onto the pommel with your inside hand and the cantle with your outside hand. This way you can pull yourself into the saddle and feel the motion in your hips and upper body.

The following exercises will help you to gain independence and suppleness in your seat:

• Ride with your eyes closed to feel how the horse moves underneath you and what your body is doing. Eliminating your ability to see what is happening will heighten your sense of feel.

• Pull yourself deep down into the saddle often by holding onto the saddle or the little front strap to experience the feeling of sitting.

• Do a mental check of which muscles are tight or loose by focusing on them separately.

• Ride without stirrups and reins and let your arms hang down loosely to the sides so that your hands lie behind your thighs. Imagine you have no legs and find your seat by balancing your upper body.

• Lay your hands on the horse's shoulders or croup and feel when each of the horse's legs is moving forward. Lay your hands on the horse's back, right behind the saddle, and feel the two sides move up and down. Say aloud what you feel ("right hind is moving forward now") and have the ground person check this. This will help you apply your aids at the right moment.

Have your seat corrected while riding with reins and stirrups as well as without them. To check how your aids are working ride up and down transitions without reins or with a person on the ground commanding the horse. This is especially useful for checking your back aid in the down transition.

After developing a basic seat and a working use of the aids on the lunge line, begin learning the arena figures, simple movements, and transitions.

GYMNASTICS FOR THE RIDER

Depending on how athletic and flexible you are (be honest with yourself), consider giving yourself a warm-up with gymnastics and stretching movements on the ground to prepare for a riding session.

Regularly doing stretches and gymnastics on the horse will increase your balance, elasticity, seat, and feeling and will be a lot of fun as well. Try the following movements while on the lunge line or free on a very reliable horse. Don't feel that you need to perfect these movements. Just use them to give your body a better feeling on the horse. You may find that your horse is uneasy while you move differently on his back. Give him time to get used to the experience; recognize that some horses are simply not good mounts for gymnastics. You can do the exercises with a saddle or bareback with a vaulting girth for a different experience.

• Circle one or both arms forward, then backward. Extend your fingers and arms and make large circles. You will feel your shoulders rolling as your arms circle. Try not to let your seat be influenced by the movement of your arms. This exercise is very helpful if you tend to collapse in the hip or stiffen in the shoulder area. It will help stretch your body, especially your spine. Try it in walk and canter.

• Place your arms behind your head or back while you sit the walk, trot, and canter. The tendency is to lean forward, so sit tall and try to keep your upper body straight.

• Put your hands on your hips and grip your hipbones. Turn your upper body sideways as far as possible, being careful not to collapse it to the side. Next, do the same rotating movement with the arms stretched out. Turn to the left and touch the horse's left side of the croup with your left hand.

Do the same to the right. Let your head turn too, while your pelvis and legs stay in correct dressage-seat position. Do this in all gaits. This exercise will help your upper body gain flexibility.

• Lean down, touch and hold onto your toes, first to one side, then to the other. Work your way down by stroking the horse from his withers down to his elbow. Don't allow your legs to move backward. This exercise will improve your balance in different positions and will strengthen your stomach and back muscles. After trying this at the walk, try it at trot and canter.

• To try the vaulting movement called the mill, turn yourself around on the horse, moving your legs over his neck and back to make a 360-degree turn. Make those turns to the left and right, staying in the ladies seat (sitting sideways but looking forward) and sitting backward for a while to get a feeling for the horse's motion and improve your own balance.

• Lean your upper body backward as far as you can until you can lie down on the horse's back. Let your arms hang down loosely. Sit up again by pressing into the saddle with the knees. Try not to let your lower legs move. This will improve your overall balance, strengthen your belly and back muscles, and stretch your thighs and hip joint.

• Lean forward and embrace the horse around the neck.

• Pull your legs up as far as possible and stretch them down again. This will strengthen your ability to balance in the seat.

• Move your legs back and forth. As a first exercise, move the legs from the thighs down. Next, move the lower legs only, so the knee joint is used. This exercise will improve your knees' flexibility and stretch your thigh muscles.

• To try the vaulting exercise called the flag, kneel on the horse with one leg, and stretch and straighten the other leg behind you, lifting it as high as possible. Lift the diagonal arm forward.

• Push both arms forward every other step in both walk and trot, while keeping your upper body erect. This exercise will help your seat become closer and heavier in the saddle.

27

• Move one leg up and over the horse's neck to sit sidesaddle. (Lay your leg on the horse's withers with the pommel in the bend of your knee.) Try it on both sides, first in the halt, then the walk. This exercise will improve the balance of your upper body.

• Loosen your ankles by rotating them, moving your feet in circles.

These are just a few possibilities for gymnastics on the horse. Besides these exercises and others that you can find in books on gymnastics or vaulting, you can always create your own. Try them in a relaxed situation without being too serious. Not only will they increase your balance, flexibility, and security, they will help you relax mentally. Being in positions other than the normal dressage or forward seat will improve your ability to handle challenges such as being on a bucking or spooking horse.

Vaulting lessons are a perfect way to introduce younger children to horses and riding. Children will learn about horses in a group situation, and the gymnastics done in vaulting will develop their balance and confidence.

4 | The Rider's Seat

The rider's seat on a horse is constantly shifting and rebalancing with a minimum of movement and tension. The rider alternately tenses and relaxes his muscles. Stand still for a moment with even weight on your legs and close your eyes. You will feel that you are moving ever so slightly to keep your body balanced over your feet.

The classical riding system teaches both the dressage seat and the forward seat as fundamentals for every beginning rider. There are many training situations in which a fluid change between the two is necessary. Both

The dressage seat

seats require relaxed and springy joints that absorb the horse's motion like a car's shocks. A supple and balanced seat allows you to use your aids correctly, independent of your body's movement.

Centered position of the pelvis

Incorrect: pelvis tilted forward

Incorrect: pelvis tilted backward

The correct position is the basis of your influence as a rider. You or your trainer should never be satisfied with an incorrect seat because it will inhibit your horse's understanding or performance. But do not get frustrated if it takes a long time to achieve a correct seat, especially if you are a beginning adult or already have some bad habits in your seat.

Classical training begins with the dressage seat and develops the forward seat at a later stage. Switching often from the dressage to the forward seat and back will develop your balance and elasticity. Frequent switching between the sitting and posting trot also will help develop your seat.

THE DRESSAGE SEAT

The foundation of the dressage seat is the position of your pelvis, which, with the seat bones and the pubic bone, forms the seat triangle.

In the correct position, the pelvis is centered. Shifting the pelvis too far forward or back makes joints lock up and muscles stiffen, and prevents you from staying with the horse's motion.

Experiment by sitting either on a horse or on a chair. Sit on the chair like you sit on a horse, with your legs on the sides.

Move your pelvis to feel what happens to the rest of your body as you shift forward and backward.

Tilt your pelvis forward by rolling over the seat bones. Touch the upper front part of the pelvis with your hands to feel the motion. Touch the vertebra of the lower back, which are buried by muscles on the right and left sides. A severe hollow back will develop, stiffening your spine. You will not be sitting on your pelvis anymore, but on the contracted muscles of the inner thigh.

Now roll back on your seat bones until your pelvis is tilted far back. You feel like you are crouching. Your back and shoulders will be rounded, your chest will collapse, and your head will move unnaturally forward with a stiffened neck. The muscle on the upper front of your thighs will tense, your knees will move upward. The pubic bone will lose contact with the saddle.

Now try the centered position of the pelvis, where the point of hip of the upper pelvis and the pubic bone are vertically aligned. In this position the back muscles slightly hide the lower vertebrae but are still supple. The legs can hang down loosely from the hip. There is no contraction of the inner thigh muscles and no tension in the knees. Keep the natural hollow in your back. If you try to straighten your spine, your back will become stiff. A centered pelvis brings the seat bones into close contact with the saddle.

As the horse moves, the supple pelvis and spine move softly back and forth to absorb motion. You may observe many other riders who swing in the waist or even the shoulders to cope with the horse's motion. As soon as you understand the pelvic movement, you and your horse will look glued together; you will become a unit.

Use the next warm-up with your horse or your next lungeing lesson to experience your pelvic movement as the horse moves. Start by letting yourself be moved by the horse's motion; do not try anything active. Feel

Correct leg and foot position

Incorrect: foot turned outward

Incorrect: foot turned inward

how the hind leg of the horse moves your seat bone forward on the same side. It feels like walking on your seat bones. Feel how your pelvis and spine are moving. When you have fully absorbed this body motion, you will be able to use it on purpose to influence the horse.

Buttocks are completely relaxed in the saddle.

To experience what your buttocks muscles do, sit on a hard chair. Spread your legs a little without tensing any muscles. Now straighten your upper body. Be careful that you do not have a hollow back! You will feel your seat bones pressing onto the chair. Now tense your buttock muscles — you will feel that they are covering the seat bones, cushioning them from below and pushing you above the chair. Tense buttocks cause you to lose influence on the horse.

The legs hang down from the relaxed hip joint. The thighs are moved back and turned inward so they rest with their wide inside on the saddle and the knees lie flat at the saddle.

Bring your thighs back as far as possible while still sitting on the seat bones and without locking the hip. This will bring the knees into a lower position that is necessary to envelop the horse and sit deep in the saddle. To sit deeply keep your thigh muscles relaxed whenever possible. As a test, tense the inner thigh muscles You will restrict the movement of the pelvis and push yourself out of the saddle.

By turning your thighs inward, you will place your leg in the correct, slightly angled position. Conversely, thighs turned outward will stretch the whole leg and cause it to stiffen.

Practice the position and feel of the thighs when sitting on the horse. Slightly spread your thighs away from the saddle, turn them inward and back, then place them on the saddle again. You may grab the backside muscles of your thighs in order to move the muscle even farther back and out from under your leg. Feel how the seat bone comes in closer contact to the saddle.

You may find that you use your thighs and knees and maybe even your calves to hold yourself on the horse. But this will not work for long. You cannot tense your muscles forever. They will tire and cramp. This "holding" prevents you from sitting with your weight and seat bones close to the horse.

However, there are some instances when pressing with your knees and thighs is appropriate. When on a bucking horse, you want to press your thighs, and especially your knees, as hard as possible to give yourself a better hold.

Sometimes a horse pulls strongly on the reins, especially in transitions, and then tenses his back so that it is hard to sit. You can avoid being pulled out of the saddle by maintaining your weight/back aid's influence on the horse by pressing slightly with your thighs and knees.

If you are starting a young horse in sitting trot and transitions, his back muscles will stay more supple and he will obey better if you press slightly with your thighs and knees in order to avoid putting your full weight onto the horse's back. This also will help you sit the uneven steps of a green horse without bouncing on his back.

The lower leg hangs down loosely with a slight bend at the knee. The flat inside of the calves keeps contact with the horse's body.

You will feel that you automatically lower your heels when you tense

Calf positioned correctly

Incorrect: Calf too far back; stirrup positioned incorrectly

Incorrect: Calf too far forward

your calf muscles and lift up your toes. Those points depend on each other. With tensed calves, you can give stronger and more controlled leg pressure and keep the calves more consistently in place.

Your knee should always have a bend so your ankles can keep their correct position, vertically underneath the hip joint. Stretching your leg straight will bring your calves away from the horse and make your seat unbalanced. Especially while rising to post, the beginner tends to stretch the leg straight to get out of the saddle. Make an effort never to stretch your leg completely in the knee joint when rising. Rise only so much that the angle in your knee opens but still exists. (For skiers, it is like coming down an uneven hill; you angle your leg in the knee a little more, a little less, but never stand up straight.)

The stirrups should be long enough so that the rider has a long leg with a low knee and heel but not too long that the knee is straight.

The correct stirrup length varies depending on your training level, your horse's level, his condition, and the exercise you are undertaking. The stirrup should be long enough that a slight lifting of your toes and the ball of your foot make it possible to slide in. The correct length will maintain the knee's angle.

Some riders prefer to keep the stirrups shorter until their own joints and muscles are warmed up and loose. Shorter stirrups are also used when training young horses and for beginning riders.

When you are learning the sitting trot and canter, riding without stirrups may help you to relax and gain a deep seat. Learning solely with stirrups often leads to the rider clinching the saddle too much while standing stiffly in the stirrups. This habit is very difficult to correct once established.

Stirrups that are too short will result in the "chair seat," which stiffens and weakens the whole seat, especially the hips, and brings the rider to push himself out of the saddle. Stirrups that are too long will produce a "fork seat." The rider will try to stretch his legs out to keep the stirrups on and consequently stiffen in his hips, sit on his thighs, and allow his legs to slide back too far. Stirrups that are too long or too short will make the rider stiffen and push incorrectly. Training young horses and preparing for cavaletti work or jumping, we take the dressage seat with slightly shorter stirrups, approximately one or two holes.

The toes are kept almost parallel to the horse or slightly outward.

You may hear your trainer say, "Put your toes in!" Every beginner tends to turn his toes too far out, which will open his knees, bringing them away from the saddle. This command will correct this tendency. Turning them in too much, however, will stiffen the whole leg.

The heels are the rider's lowest body part. The ankle stays supple to absorb the rider's weight.

Tensed calf muscles and lifted toes will lower the heels and make the ankle springy. This will provide a long leg and a low knee so that you can embrace your horse with your seat and legs. To feel a springy ankle, stand on the edge of a stair on the balls of your feet and toes. Slightly bend your knees and let your heels move up and down by being elastic in the ankle. You want the same motion when you are riding.

Correct upper body

Keep the stirrups under the ball of the foot so the ankle can flex.

If you push your feet too far into the stirrups, you will immobilize the ankle, which will prevent it from being elastic enough to absorb your weight. It would also prevent all other leg joints from being elastic. In a correctly built and fitted saddle, the stirrup leather is attached to the saddle so that the stirrup automatically falls underneath the ball of your foot. When your ankle is positioned correctly underneath the hip joint, you should be able to release the stirrup without changing its position. If the stirrup moves back or forth when released, your lower leg is either too far back or forward. This test is a great exercise for self-control. Lift the toes only slightly to release the stirrup. Otherwise the knees will pull up. You will find this game helpful if you are afraid of losing a stirrup. Practice it both while standing still and while your horse is in motion.

Incorrect: the rider overarches the chest

Incorrect: the rider hollows the chest

Head is upright and centered

The upper body comes up straight out of the hips and is vertical to the horse's back. The upper body has enough tension to maintain the position but with the elasticity to swing and to absorb the horse's motion. The hips stay equal height above the saddle.

It is important to sit erect but supple. Hollowing the back will stiffen the whole seat and make it impossible for your hips to swing. Hunching forward will do the same. You will lose balance and stability. In both incorrect positions you lose the accuracy of your aids.

A controlled and correct upper body is essential for your ability to swing in the pelvis along with the horse's motion. The chest must be held correctly to allow this movement. To arch the chest sufficiently, lift the breastbone so it is vertical. Experience this at the walk. Let yourself swing with the horse's motion. You can put a hand on the breastbone. Feel how the pelvis changes position while swinging, how the sternum lifts and lowers slightly, and how your spine moves.

Now try the feel when your chest and upper body collapse, as well as when you take an exaggerated upright and stiffened position. A common mistake in the effort to sit upright and swing is to make the whole upper body swing back and forth.

The shoulders are held loosely and back far enough to arch the chest.

Take a deep breath. You will feel your rib cage expand, the breastbone lift, and your whole upper body rise. Breathing deeply helps straighten the upper body.

The head is kept upright and centered over the body; eyes are looking forward.

Hold your head upright and centered without tensing your neck. Look through the horse's ears and be aware of your environment.

If you look down, keep your chin too far forward or backward, or tilt your head, you will negatively influence the posture of your whole upper body. The upper body will stiffen; shoulders and thighs will tense; the chest will collapse, restricting your breathing; your weight may shift incorrectly; and your ability to "swing" with the horse's motion will be restricted.

The upper arms hang down loosely from the shoulder and almost in a vertical line. The arm is angled forward at the elbow, which is held firmly to the body together with the lower inside arm.

Keep your elbow and lower arm leaning on your body, but not so tightly that your muscles become tense. Do not hold your elbows away from the body. This creates stiff and shaking arms and hands, which are hard on the horse's mouth.

To have a soft, quiet hand position, keep the arms bent and flexible in the elbow. Stretched-out arms are stiff and inflexible. Try the feeling of bent and stretched arms briefly when you ride next time. You will feel the difference.

Correct hands

The hands are closed into fists without tensing. They are carried in an upright position, with the slightly angled thumb on top. The wrists are not bent in normal position. They are kept a small hand's width above the horse's withers and apart from each other.

Correct hands

For correct height, the rider keeps his fists so that an unbroken line could be drawn from the horse's mouth through the rein and lower arm, visible from the side and from above. This "invisible" line is an important checkpoint. The height of the rider's hands depends on the height of the horse's mouth. The proper space between your fists depends on the width of your horse's neck. The distance generally is about a small hand's width, but whatever the distance, the straight line from horse's mouth through rein and lower arm should be maintained.

Incorrect: hands too low

Close your fists just hard enough to keep the reins from sliding through your hands. Do not tense and close your fists too tightly or your rein aids will become too strong and your arms tense. If your hands are twisted in the

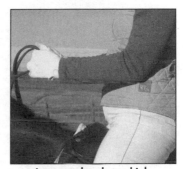

Incorrect: hands too high

wrist, your hands will get stiff and unmovable. Sensitive rein aids are then impossible.

The rider takes the reins between the small finger and the ring finger into the fist. The hands must be able to act independently from the rest of the body.

The reins leave the fist lying on the forefinger with the thumb resting angled on top, looking like a roof. The reins should be of even length to start with and not twisted. Excess reins should hang down on the right side of the horse's neck below the rein leading to the horse's mouth.

You should be able to draw two lines when you watch a dressage seat.

The first is a vertical line from ear over shoulder over hip down to the heel. The second line runs from the elbow over lower arm, fist, and rein to the horse's mouth. This same line must also be visible from above.

MISTAKES IN THE DRESSAGE SEAT

To obtain a supple and balanced seat that moves in unison with the horse, we have to evaluate the reasons for certain mistakes to correct them. Always make sure that a poorly fitted saddle is not the culprit. Correction by a trainer, lungeing lessons concentrating on seat, and gymnastics to achieve more suppleness throughout your whole dressage training will be invaluable.

Mistakes in the seat will always occur, and they happen to everybody at some point, but correcting them early is important. Every mistake that becomes a bad habit is more difficult to break.

The chair seat: The chair seat can result from stirrups that are too short

Chair seat

or a saddle with the deepest point too far back. The chair seat gets its name from its look, with the rider sitting on the horse like on a chair.

When you sit too far back in the saddle, you will not be able to sit on your seat bones, a hunched back develops, and your ability to swing in the lower spine will be compromised. Your head and arms will shift forward, producing stiff elbows and shaking hands. In the chair seat, your buttock muscles are tensed, thighs and knees are pulled up, and the stirrups slide forward. The calves are too far forward and cannot give correct aids. The rider holds the reins too tightly because he is so unbalanced and behind the horse's motion.

Move your seat into the center and lowest point of the saddle. Stretch the whole body so that your torso straightens and your legs lengthen. Arch your chest out more. Always check for the vertical line connecting ear, shoulder, hip, and heel. Your stirrups may need to be lengthened.

The fork seat: Sitting too much on your thighs and crotch with little weight on the seat bones can result from stirrups that are too long or a saddle with the deepest point too far forward.

Fork seat

If your inner thigh muscles have to bear your weight, they cannot stay relaxed. Your whole leg, especially the lower leg, will slide back too far and your ankles will be stiff; your feet will lose the stirrups again and again. It is common to develop a hollow back, which prevents the spine from swinging, which in turn prevents a supple seat. Correct weight aids are impossible because the buttocks and seat bones are not in contact with the saddle and the calves do not have much force.

Try holding your body with less muscle tension and shifting your weight from your thighs onto your seat bones. Move your upper body back. The stirrups may need to be shortened.

Stirrup sits wrong: Your feet are too far into the stirrups. You get stiff and rigid in the ankle and leg, and your knees come up. Keep the stirrup under the ball of your foot. This way your ankle can be springy to absorb your weight. Your knee will stay low, your calf quiet.

Pulled up or open knee: You squeeze too hard with your thighs so your heels draw up. Stretch your leg down, keep the thigh muscles loose, and turn thigh and knee inward to contact the horse with the knees' flat side.

Stiff, tensed hips/pelvis: With a tense pelvis you will bounce in the saddle, which will be uncomfortable for you and the horse. Try to let your pelvis swing with the horse's rhythm. Ride the walk and concentrate on developing a swinging, following seat, then transfer this feeling to the trot and canter. Try holding onto the points of your hip bones with your hands while at the walk and let the horse just take you forward. You will feel your pelvis automatically move. This motion is essential to understand.

Elbows spread away from the body and shake: This happens to a lot of beginners when starting with the sitting trot. The moving elbows make the hands shake, too, bothering the horse's mouth. Try keeping your arms in contact with your body to avoid this.

Elbows pressed on the body too strongly: This, too, will make your hands stiff and shaky and your shoulders and upper body tense. Keep your arms next to your body but in a relaxed way so that your arms can swing in the elbows.

Hands shaking up and down severely: One reason for shaking hands is a seat not yet supple enough to absorb the horse's motion in the pelvis, spine, and joints, which makes the rider bounce on the horse and therefore influences the hands. Keeping your arm straight in the elbow joint can also cause shaky hands. A stiff, straight arm has no flexibility to adapt to motion because the joint locks up in this position. Angle your elbow and learn to be elastic. The arm needs to stretch and bend rhythmically to keep the hands in the same position at all times.

Pulled up shoulders: These make the arms and hands stiff or shake. Your upper body will stiffen, too. When you feel this happen, move your shoulders up and down a few times to get the tension out of them, until you feel that they are really hanging loosely.

Upper body too far back: This will make you stiff, and you probably will bounce and pull too much. It often happens when you want to increase the verticality of the upper body or concentrate on swinging.

Chest sunken in: This happens when you sit in a hunched position with rounded shoulders, a collapsed chest, and your head tilted down. The upper body lacks stability, affecting the entire body. Take a few long, deep breaths and you will feel how your chest comes out and forward and the necessary basic muscle tone develops in the upper body. This is especially important in transitions. I often suggest that my students feel arrogant and proud while riding, which helps them assume the right position automatically.

Stiffened neck: In order to sit upright you may stiffen your neck muscles and maybe even shift your whole head forward or backward. Try to be aware of the stiffened muscles. Shift your head forward and back a few times to release the muscle, then center it.

Moving one fist sideways over the withers: The horse receives incorrect commands from the hands and tends to shorten his neck too much and tilt in the poll. This often happens when the rider forgets to shorten the rein for a new situation.

Reins too long: If the reins are too long, you will have to pull too much to have any influence. Your elbows will be stiff and too far back. Correct the length of rein.

Head looking down: You may find yourself watching the horse's head and neck or your hands. This will negatively influence your whole body's posture, especially the weight and back aid. Rely on feeling what is going on and do not move your head down so much when looking.

Open fingers

Fists opened too much: If your hands aren't closed the reins will slide through your fists, which will cause you to begin pulling to shorten them. The constant pulling will bother the horse. You may find that your fists end up too close to your belly. Also the rider tends to shorten the reins so often that he dis-

Covered fists

turbs the horse with unsteady contact. If you are not quite aware that your reins slide through your fingers, temporarily mark the reins at one or a few places with colored tape. This makes a change in rein length more visible, and you may be able to correct it quicker.

Covered fists or those bent too much and stiff to the inside or outside: The rider keeps the fist turned in so that the knuckles are on top instead of the thumb. This will make your fists stiff and therefore your rein aids will be too harsh or abrupt. Because a rein aid out of the wrist is not possible, the rider gives his rein aids by moving the whole arm or even the upper body. Return to the correct position with your hands and then feel that they are not kept tense. Only from a correct hand position can you give correct and soft rein aids. In the beginning, riders tend to use too much strength, making a fist out of the hand so the reins will not slip through. This will build up too much tenseness. Find the right amount.

Heels drawn up: This will change your whole leg position. When your heels are drawn up, your knees will come up, too. Your thighs tense, whereas the calf muscles will lose the necessary tension they need. Heels drawn up prevent the ankle from moving slightly up and down to absorb the rider's weight. This can result from stirrups that are too long or the mere attempt to push a very lazy horse.

Collapsing to one side: This often happens in turns, bending work, lateral movements, when starting the canter, or whenever the upper body must follow the direction of a movement. When you drop a shoulder, your weight will shift to the side opposite the collapsing one and influence your horse incorrectly. It is most common for a rider to collapse to the inside while riding a bent line or trying to put weight on the inside seat bone. Try to straighten your upper body. If you have an arena equipped with mirrors, use them to correct yourself when riding alone. Ride lines that lead toward the mirror so you can see if your shoulders are the same height. Moving toward the mirror on the arena's long side on the bend line of a circle is the best exercise, as we tend to collapse more on bend lines. When riding turns, concentrate on rotating your upper body into the direction of the turn, the inside shoulder moving slightly backward and the outside shoulder forward. This will shift your weight intensely on your inside seat bone.

Losing balance: The rider who loses balance, and therefore suppleness, commonly reacts with several reflexes to regain balance. His legs start clinging to the horse and his hands pull back. In extreme cases, this clinging reflex combined with fear can evoke the "fetal crouch reflex" in a rider. This ancient defensive human reflex is the worst thing we can do on a horse. It makes the horse uncomfortable,

Collapsing to one side

nervous, and may frighten him, too. He loses his own rhythm and suppleness and becomes tense. To avoid the uncomfortable rider, he'll either get lazy or he may start rushing. A fearful rider needs to be aware of what he is doing in order to stop doing it. A comfortable routine, as well as diversion, will decrease fear and reduce the occurrence of those defensive reflexes.

You need to keep your balance without tension or stiffness and without holding yourself on the horse with pure muscle strength. You want to achieve a supple flow with the horse's motion first, then bring every part of the body into the correct position. This means your brain has to command your body to alternate between tensing and relaxing muscles. Never forget to listen to your body and check if the right muscles are tensed as much as necessary and if others are relaxed and supple. It may take awhile because you may have never used some of the muscles this way.

You and your trainer must consider your physique, as well as the horse's height and the width of his rib cage, when determining your correct position. These factors will cause slight deviations from the ideal seat but shouldn't be used as an excuse for an incorrect position.

THE FORWARD SEAT

In Germany, the forward seat is taught only after the rider has learned the dressage seat. The purpose of the forward seat is to remove your weight from the horse's back and move your center of gravity forward with the motion of the horse in higher speed.

You will use a forward seat to keep your weight off a young horse's back when starting him in dressage. The forward seat is also more comfortable for trail riding at a gallop and is used when doing cavaletti work (going over elevated ground poles and small jumps). We always use it for canter at high speed on longer distances and during jumping and trail riding.

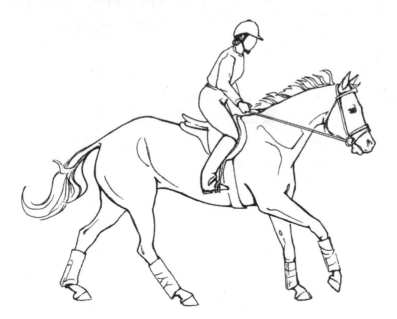

Forward seat

Differences from the dressage seat

The buttocks are not in the saddle but lifted a little above. The greater the speed of the horse, the higher you should lift. This will shift your weight off your buttocks and the horse's back and onto your thighs and knees. Stand strong in the stirrups and hold onto the horse's sides with your thigh and knee muscles. Balance your weight on your thighs and knees. The horse will feel your weight more on his sides than on his vertebrae and back muscles.

You will need to shorten the stirrups three to five holes to maintain a stable position. This allows you to distribute your weight differently on the horse and gives a stable position. You can put your foot a little farther into the stirrup to have better support and to keep the lower leg quiet. The shorter stirrup produces greater angles in the hip and knee joints. Because of the increased angle, the knees will sit farther forward on the saddle.

A dressage saddle is impractical for the forward seat because it is not possible to shorten the stirrups enough without the knee moving in front of the saddle flaps.

Move your upper body forward between one and two hand widths, depending on the speed, situation, and movement you are undertaking with the horse. Lean forward out of your hip joint with the vertebrae kept straight. As your hands move closer to the horse's mouth, you will need to shorten the reins.

The weight/back aid is not used in the forward seat. But if you are not too high above the saddle with your buttocks and want to use it for transitions to a slower or higher speed or for small turns, you just sit down again and use it briefly. Depending on the situation, you keep the upper body leaning slightly forward or bring it back to the vertical when needed.

For short-term use of the forward seat during dressage sessions, you need not shorten the stirrups as much.

When learning the forward seat or riding in it for long periods, a "rein bridge" will allow you to lean on the rein when necessary and help you keep your balance. To make a rein bridge, take the rein coming from the left between the thumb and forefinger and into your right hand. The rein between both hands should be about 8 inches long. The piece of rein between your hands will lie on the horse's withers. Hold it in place on both sides of the withers with your thumbs and allow a constant contact to the horse's mouth.

5 | Gaits and How to Ride Them

In dressage, the horse's gaits are walk, trot, and canter. To be able to give your aids properly, you need to know the sequence of the horse's footfalls.

In each gait we have several tempos, which differ in the amount of collection and the length of stride. To be correct, each pace has to be in perfect rhythm.

THE WALK

The walk has a four-beat rhythm. Because there is no moment of suspension in walk, we do not have impulsion. When a front leg moves forward, the diagonal hind leg follows. When a hind leg moves forward, the front leg on the same side — called the lateral front leg — follows. Example: right front/left hind/left front/right hind. The horse should walk with long, eager, and rhythmic strides.

The pace is a gait similar to walk; "gaited" horse breeds generally are born with the pace in addition to walk, trot, and canter. In dressage it is considered a fault. Horses that naturally have a very good walk with a big overstride may tend to switch to the pace, mainly when the rider's influence is not careful enough. The rider may drive the horse forward too strongly and cause him to rush, resulting in pacing instead of walking. Or the rider, usually in addition to the overly driving leg aid, restrains the horse too much with the reins and too many influencing cues.

Observe a walking horse from the side. The horse's lateral pair of legs form a "V" between them when the hind leg swings forward and almost touches the front leg before it moves forward. At the pace, the lateral pair of legs moves forward simultaneously; we cannot see the "V."

The main faults in walk are the switch to pace and hurried steps, which eventually change to a jig. Bringing the horse on the bit too early in his training can cause a "bad" walk. Only a very sensitive and experienced rider will be able to correct this while riding walk on the bit. He will temporarily slow down speed in the walk and use all aids to bring the horse back into a quiet four-beat rhythm. The less experienced rider must ride more often on a loose or long rein at a rather slow and quiet speed to let the horse find his rhythm again. Additional help to correct the walk are walking calmly on trail rides, up hills, over cavaletti, and riding walk in the arena, switching into slight leg-yields or shoulder-ins in between walk stretches.

It is an old truism in dressage riding that the walk is the most difficult gait to ride. Because of the lack of suspension and impulsion, the walk is more difficult to improve and easier to destroy.

The different tempos of the walk

Medium walk: This is the horse's natural walk. The horse's hind leg should step a little over the track of the front leg. Keep contact with the horse's mouth, allowing the slight nodding in head and neck.

Extended walk: In the extended walk, the horse's steps cover more ground, although the extent depends on the horse's natural ability and conformation. The hind legs should step at least one hoof width over the track of the front leg or at least farther than in the horse's medium walk. While you need to maintain contact with the bit, your hands need to give a little more rein to allow the horse's frame to lengthen.

Collected walk: In the collected walk, the horse covers less ground in each step than in the medium walk. The hind legs step into the track of the front leg or stay a little behind. As in every collected gait, the forehand lifts and the haunches lower. The horse's head comes closer to the vertical. The horse stays eager; his steps are more elevated.

Leg aids for the walk

To encourage good movement at the walk, we want to engage the hind legs, which are the horse's motor. Push with one of your legs at a time (so you have a left-right-left-right order). Your left leg needs to push the instant the horse's left hind leg is extending forward.

To find the right moment to push, ride your horse in a free walk on a loose rein. Have him move forward very energetically so that you are able to feel his motion. You may need to use a crop to drive him forward or have somebody help from the ground in order to keep your leg free to feel. When it is safe, close your eyes so you can concentrate on feeling. Relax your legs and let them hang down, but keep contact with the horse's body with your calves. The moment your horse is moving his left hind leg forward, you will feel the left side of his back lowering. You will feel your left seat bone drop down as much as the horse's back lowers. At the same instant, your left leg will swing toward the horse's body. As the horse moves his right hind leg forward, you will experience the same with your right leg and seat bone.

To drive your horse forward at the walk, push at the exact moment that your leg swings toward the horse's body. If you let your body feel for it, the right moment comes very naturally. Give as much leg pressure as is needed to assist your horse to perform optimally.

Rein aids for the walk

To achieve a good walk, it is necessary to allow the horse's natural nodding motion of the head and neck. You will find this motion very visible in young horses, less visible in horses at higher levels of training, and most pronounced in the free walk of all horses. The horse is stretching and contracting his neck and back muscles, which work together with the muscles of his hind legs. If you restrict or interfere with that motion, the horse will walk with short steps and a tense back. Whenever you ride with a shorter rein and have contact with the horse's mouth, you must swing your hands slightly back and forth to allow the horse the freedom to move his head and neck. Use your hands and arms as if they are rubber bands; stretch and contract to follow the horse's nodding, but still maintain pressure to feel the contact with the horse's mouth to give rein aids.

Weight/back aids for the walk

It is easy to sit the walk because there is no suspension. However, you still influence with your weight and back aid. At the walk on a straight line, keep your body weight balanced equally on both seat bones. The danger in the slow movement of walk is that you may drop one seat bone (and therefore put more weight on it) the moment the horse lowers this side of his back while the hind leg swings forward. This way you are using your weight unintentionally and probably at the wrong moment. Sit upright on the horse and swing forward with your hips, going with the horse's motion. When you swing more actively and use a stronger pushing leg aid and following hands, you will increase the length of stride and make the walk more powerful (example: free walk).

Slowing the activity of your hips by swinging your hips more passively together with a more careful but still pushing leg and a slightly restraining rein aid will achieve a more calm or collected walk. Do not forget you can only change your back aid as much as you still move in rhythm with the horse's motion.

THE TROT

The trot is a two-beat rhythm with impulsion. The horse is moving his diagonal pair of legs forward simultaneously followed by a moment of suspension. Then the other diagonal pair of legs steps on the ground and extends forward followed by another moment of suspension. Example: left front and right hind/suspension/right front and left hind/suspension.

As in every gait, rhythm and an even length of stride with enough impulsion of the hind legs are important. The trot is the easiest gait to keep in rhythm.

The different tempos in trot

All paces in trot should have a clear two-beat rhythm, good suspension, and enough impulsion.

Working trot: The working trot is the average trot pace of the horse. It is an eager pace in which the well-engaged hind legs step into the track of the front leg.

Medium trot: In a medium trot, the hind legs step over the track of the front leg and the horse moves in a longer frame. The horse stays in contact and has self-carriage. In some of the lower-level dressage tests, a "lengthening of the strides" is required. This is a preliminary stage to the medium trot, allowing a gradual progression from the working trot to the medium trot. In the medium trot, the horse has to gain more length of stride without getting into a quicker rhythm. The stronger impulsion of the hind legs gives the front legs more freedom to lengthen.

Extended trot: The extended trot is the fullest extension of the movement described in medium trot. The hind legs step farther over the front legs' track, and the horse is allowed into an even longer frame. To perform an extended trot, the horse's hindquarters must have been strengthened by collected work.

Collected trot: In the collected trot, the hind legs

Working trot

Medium trot

Collected trot

step farther under the horse's center of gravity while having a stronger bend and more active haunches. The horse's stride will shorten without reducing his eagerness, activity, and impulsion. The horse's forehand will lift and lighten, which will shift more weight to the hindquarters. The trot steps will become more elevated and cadenced. At the most, the hind legs step into the track of the front leg.

The aids for the trot

To start the trot out of halt or the walk, give leg pressure on both sides simultaneously whenever one of the diagonal pairs of legs extends forward. This moment is easy to identify because you can see it well. At the trot, one hind leg extends at exactly the same moment as the diagonal front leg. As you see the front leg extend, you will feel your hips swing forward and simultaneously you give leg pressure.

Sitting the trot is one of the most difficult things to learn in riding, especially for adult riders. Nevertheless, it is essential. A correct but supple body posture and seat will enable your horse to perform to his optimum. A good way to improve your sitting trot is to practice riding without stirrups.

You sit with an upright upper body with all your weight in the saddle. The beginner feels like he is being thrown up and down in the saddle, which is very uncomfortable. That happens because of the horse's suspension during trot. Now you need to learn to "sit" the trot. For this, let us remember our experiences in the walk. Here you could already feel how the horse's motion moves your pelvis rhythmically forward. Now you not only let this happen, but you do it on purpose and more strongly in the trot to absorb the up-and-down movement with your pelvis and spine. Your pelvis and spine have the same function as shocks in a car.

To swing elastically in the trot, the spine needs to be in a natural upright position. The body center must be supple and elastic to allow swinging. Pelvis and upper body must be supple, having just the right amount of muscle tension to allow the pelvis to swing with the horse's motion. We reach the slight pelvis motion by using the belly and lower back muscles.

Most of this muscle work happens through reflexes to keep balance. The lesser part happens through actively induced muscle work.

Split the horse's trot into the separate moments to see what exactly happens: The horse's back swings up and down in the trot. When the back lifts, the rider slightly contracts belly and lower back muscles. This tilts the lower pelvis forward. The next moment the horse's back lowers. The rider releases the contraction of belly and lower back muscles. The lower part of the pelvis moves back. The motion must be within the horse's rhythm of motion.

The beginner needs to do this muscle movement deliberately; the advanced rider does it mostly automatically. A basic amount of muscle tension in the whole body is necessary to sit the trot. The rider will stiffen and bounce when he tenses the muscles too much. The rider also bounces when he keeps his body too loose.

Posting or rising trot

We use posting trot to start young horses, to warm up, and when we trot on trail rides. The beginning rider usually learns the posting trot first because it diminishes the negative influence of the rider's weight on the horse's back. The posting trot is a mixture of putting weight on and off the horse's back with the seat. Rise from the saddle when one diagonal pair of legs of the horse extends forward. To rise, press your thighs and knees slightly against the horse to gain support. Put more weight in your stirrups, standing slightly on the ball of the foot, and raise your buttocks a little off the saddle while pushing your hips forward. Keep your ankles springy to absorb your motion.

Rise the moment the outside front leg of the horse is extending forward (it moves simultaneously with the inside hind leg, but this is much more difficult to feel or see). It is not necessary to go up very high — a little is enough to avoid that tossed-up feeling the horse gives you in suspension. The knees always stay bent; only their angle changes with rising or sitting. One common beginner's mistake is going up too high, which takes too much muscle power and stiffens your motion. Another common error is trying to straighten your leg when going up, which stiffens your knees and ankles. You will lose your balance, your correct leg position, and the contact between your calves and the horse's body.

Keep your upper body erect and as still as possible. The upper body should move forward just as much as necessary for you to balance correctly. The degree of leaning forward depends on the training stage of the horse and the rider's own body proportions. The vertical line of the dressage seat — head, shoulder, hip, heel — changes to head, shoulder, hip, and ball of the foot. This way you will balance your weight on your thighs, knees, and feet. Especially when you are riding with shorter stirrups, you may lean forward slightly to stay in harmony with the horse's motion.

Avoid raising your hands during the up portion of the rising trot. This results from a tense elbow joint, which will inhibit your arm from stretching and bending along with the up and down of the posting trot motion. A good way to work on this common mistake is to hold onto the little leather strap often attached to the saddle front with your little fingers to feel how your elbow angle must change during rising trot.

Common mistakes are leaning too far forward when rising and leaning backward when sitting down. Both make the rider lose balance, and a controlled up and down is not possible. Experiment with sitting down in a chair and getting up again. Move your upper body either far forward or backward during the stages and feel what happens. In addition, when the upper body leans too far forward, the buttocks move backward, and the rider will not have a weight aid anymore when sitting down.

You do not need stirrups to post properly. Take the stirrups and leathers off the saddle while you do this or cross them over the horse's shoulder right in front of the pommel so they lie on the opposite sides on his shoulder. You generally perform the exact same motion as when posting with stirrups but now need to press on the horse's sides much more strongly with thighs and knees to rise from the saddle.

Posting on the inside hind leg

Riding in an arena, the rider sits down in the saddle the moment the horse's inside hind leg steps on the ground. We say the rider posts on the inside hind leg. When this leg takes off to extend forward, you rise from the saddle. The beginner easily sees the right moment and rises the moment the horse's outside front leg extends.

Why do we post on the inside hind leg and not differently?

When riding the dressage horse on bent lines, you want to engage his inside hind leg to extend energetically, take more weight, and stay underneath the weight. You can engage the inside hind leg best when going down into the saddle and pushing. Your leg and back aids will be available at this moment.

Changing the posting when changing lead

We learned that the rider must sit down on the inside hind leg. It is obvious that the rider needs to change posting when changing direction in a riding arena because the inside hind leg of the horse changes.

To change posting, remember what you just learned: rise when the outside front leg extends, then you sit down. Here, instead of standing up again, you remain seated in the saddle for another moment — two steps or an even number of steps — then rise again. So you sit down, count one, two, rise, and observe that you are doing this when the horse's other front leg extends. You changed posting.

While posting, we keep our weight more off the horse's back. However, we still sit down in between, and we put more weight on one diagonal pair of legs. To keep an even weight distribution on all legs, we change posting in a riding arena when we change direction. We do not have any rules for trail rides, but it is still good for the horse when you change posting periodically to distribute weight evenly on the horse.

When might you want to post on "the wrong diagonal"

While you post, the influence of your weight as you sit will engage the inside hind leg more and cause this leg to swing forward a little in the direction of this diagonal. When starting the training of a green horse, you can use these circumstances to your advantage.

The green horse often has trouble picking up canter from the trot. On a large circle or in a corner, try posting on the "wrong diagonal." The outside hind leg will now have a tendency toward the inside, enabling a kind of inside bend. We cannot ask for much flexion and bend of the young horse early in training because it would disrupt more than help. It would require too many aids the green horse isn't used to yet, and trying to flex can cause the horse to resist. Posting on the wrong diagonal will help a green horse slide softly into the right canter.

When you are working a horse that has a shorter stride with one of his front legs, posting on this diagonal for a while can help even the strides.

Additionally, you can improve every horse's natural crookedness by posting on the diagonal that will encourage the crooked side's hind leg to step under the weight.

THE CANTER

The canter is a gait with impulsion and suspension and a three-beat rhythm. The canter begins with the outside hind leg, followed by the diagonal pair of inside hind and outside front legs moving together. The inside front leg then extends. A moment of suspension occurs in the canter.

The horse should have a clear three-beat rhythm with a distinctive moment of suspension. The hind legs should stride under the center of gravity as far as possible. Canter is the only gait in which we can keep an inside bend on a straight line.

The different paces of canter

Working canter: Like the medium walk and the working trot, the working canter is the standard canter pace for the beginning rider. In the working canter, the horse moves eagerly, straight, and with impulsion. With each canter stride, the horse gains about one body length of distance.

Medium canter: In the medium canter, the horse's strides lengthen and cover more ground than in a working canter. The preliminary stage to the medium canter in lower-level tests is the "lengthening of the canter strides" with a gradual development of longer strides.

Extended canter: In the extended canter, the horse covers the maximum amount of ground with even contact on the reins and a lengthened frame. The strides get longer than in medium canter, but the rhythm does not quicken. To perform an extended canter, the horse must be prepared with collected canter work.

Collected canter

Collected canter: The hind legs take more weight and move more under the center of gravity with stronger bent haunches. The stride gets more elevated and gains less ground than the working canter.

The aids for the canter

To canter properly is a challenge for the beginner. When learning, try to use a horse that does good canter departs and has a rhythmic, controllable canter. Try following these suggestions while being lunged so that you can concentrate only on yourself.

First focus on feeling how to sit and shift your weight. Next, learn your leg aids, then try using the reins and asking for bend.

Whether you are on a straight or a bent line, you need to bend your horse to the inside to start the canter. In this case, inside means the left side for the left-lead canter and right for the right-lead canter, no matter where the inside of the arena is. When it is difficult for the rider or the horse to start the canter and get the inside bend, try the canter depart from a corner. This gives the horse "natural" bend and balance on the correct side.

First get your horse supple and concentrated with cues. Shift your weight onto the inside seat bone. Bring your outside calf about one hand's width back to take a guarding position. The final impulse will be the pressure from the inside calf while shifting your inside hip slightly forward. The moment you give the inside leg pressure, cue or hold soft pressure on the outside rein and release pressure on the inside rein. While doing this, the outside leg should maintain a restraining contact to the horse's body.

During the canter, sit and give your aids the same way you did to begin the gait. In the dressage seat, you will have your back and weight in the saddle at all times. You will swing with your hips to absorb the up-and-down motion of the horse. It feels as if you are "wiping" the saddle from back to front. Your buttocks are going with the motion without moving on the saddle surface. Keep a constant rhythm with your hips. Enforcing the rhythm or slowing your own movement slightly can tell the horse to extend strides, stay impulsive and eager, collect, or prepare for a down transition to the trot or walk.

During canter on bent lines, put more weight on your inside seat bone and move this side's hip forward into the motion. The more highly trained your horse, the more you can influence with this aid. The main forward-driving leg is always the inside one. With each starting canter stride, give new leg pressure at the same moment your hips swing forward. Again, use the outside leg as a guarding leg aid. Give pressure when starting the canter or whenever necessary during the canter to keep the horse's hindquarters from drifting to the outside. Keep the horse bent around the inside leg in the canter depart and on the line you want to ride.

During all canter work, keep the horse bent to the inside. You have achieved enough bend when you can see a little of the horse's inside eye. When riding on bent lines, move your outside shoulder slightly forward to keep your upper body in unison with the bent horse.

How can you see if the horse is in a left-lead or right-lead canter?

The inside lateral pair of legs always extends in front of the outside legs. It is best to concentrate on the inside front leg. It will step farther forward than the outside front. When you are on the horse, you will be able to feel an unwanted counter — and therefore "wrong" — canter because your seat will feel wrong and stiff. You can also watch the horse's inside shoulder (you probably can see part of the leg, too). It will move later than the other one. When counter canter occurs unintentionally, it is called "false canter."

Counter canter

In the beginning, horse and rider should canter only on the true lead. This means left-lead canter going to the left and the same for the right side. At higher levels, we start to ride counter canter intentionally for collected work and to straighten the horse. In counter canter, the horse canters on the left lead going to the right and vice versa. One way to introduce the counter canter is to begin on the true lead, left, for example, then change direction through a half-circle on the long side. You return to the track on the left lead while cantering to the right. You can also do a counter canter by departing into it from a trot or walk on the long side. For example, going to the left you pick up the right lead. As the horse becomes more advanced, you can obtain the counter canter with a flying lead change. We always ride counter canter in collection and with an inside flexion of the horse's head and neck. This means in the left-lead canter we flex the horse to the left, in the right-lead canter we flex the horse to the right.

What is a "disunited" canter?

A horse that is still weak in his muscles, very sensitive, or receiving incorrect aids from the rider may start or switch to a "disunited canter" in which he switches the order of his hind legs. Pulling too much on the horse's head and neck with the inside rein — instead of rhythmic cueing — and not using the guarding outside rein and leg can bring a horse so much out of balance that the hind drifts to the outside and then switches the order of footfalls of the hind.

Some young horses have a natural tendency toward disunited canter. They are unbalanced under the rider and probably still very weak in their back and hind muscles. Work very patiently and correctly on big lines. Very often these horses have a good natural ability for flying changes later.

What is a "four-beat" canter?

The so-called "four-beat canter" is a mistake in which the diagonal pair of legs (inside hind and outside front) do not move forward simultaneously. The inside hind steps on the ground and extends, followed by the outside front leg. This often happens when the rider tries to collect the horse using aids that slow the horse without engaging the hind end or by using too much of a restraining rein. You may also see this in very lazy horses.

6 | The Aids

THE FEELING

Although much of the information in this book is defined, measured, ordered, and prescribed in a detailed step-by-step way, the most important thing to learn cannot be taught or defined or measured. It is the ability to feel that will make you a better rider and horseperson.

Achieving more and more feeling in handling the horse, giving the aids with your body, and anticipating and solving situations should be a continuous part of your training. You will learn from the already-trained horse, through your trainer's explanations, and by experimentation and testing. Every rider is different, and each one will have his own aptitude for achieving the feeling for the horse and riding. Those who are adaptable, intuitive, and sensitive with the aids will learn to truly communicate with the horse. Your physical elasticity and coordination will help you achieve "feel."

"Feeling" means to learn from the horse's reactions to your aids, to anticipate mistakes, disobedience, and hyper reactions, as well as to respond with the right amount of aids. The good rider can feel if the horse is tired or resistant. A book about the theory of riding and training can teach the complete system of what, how, and when to use the aids and suggest the intensity and amount of certain actions. However, theory can only give hints about the right feeling. The rider will explore his own body and be able to use it correctly and give aids not like a robot but intuitively at the right moment and strength. We can learn dressage theory and then gain the feel for using it to have a harmonious communication with the horse. Theory is the basis, and feeling makes the rider successful and good.

THE RIDER'S AIDS

Aids are your signals to the horse, the language with which you can communicate your wishes and commands. The combined use of the weight/back aids, the leg aids, and the rein aids will bring the horse into the desired gait, speed, and position.

In addition, we can use voice, a whip, and spurs.

We can divide the rider's aids into the following categories:

Weight/back aids:

1. Keep weight on both seat bones equally.
2. Put weight on one of the seat bones.
3. Take all the weight off the horse's back.

Leg aids:

1. The forward-driving leg
2. The sideways-pushing leg
3. The guarding (supporting) leg (partly pushing).

All of the above are driving aids except taking weight off the horse's back.

Rein aids:

1. To give rein (release pressure)
2. To take rein (take pressure)
3. To maintain, restrain (hold pressure)
4. To give direction
5. To guard, to support (keeping flexion and bend).

All are restraining aids, except the giving rein.

This section explains each aid separately. Nevertheless, we always use some combination of the weight/back aid, the leg aid, and the rein aid. The forward-driving aids are more important than the restraining aids. This means you always use driving aids before you restrain too much. The physical power to push with the leg, the amount of pressure on the rein, and the intensity of the swinging pelvis needed for the different aids depends on the horse's sensitivity, his training, and the effect or movement you want to achieve. Whenever situations occur in which you need to influence with strong aids, try to come back to soft ones as soon as possible to keep the horse sensitive and responsive. The goal is a horse that responds to almost invisible aids so that an observer could assume that the horse is responding to the rider's thoughts. Be careful not to get too "handy" — humans always think their hands are their best tool. This is not true in riding.

HOW TO USE THE AIDS

The weight/back aid

When placed incorrectly, an adult rider's weight can be very uncomfortable. Think of carrying a backpack. Packed well, you can carry it for a long time. The weight is distributed evenly and does not bounce around. Packed badly, you quickly feel uncomfortable and sore.

As you learned about the dressage and forward seats, you should begin by sitting in the saddle with your buttocks equally weighted on the two seat bones (see chapter 4). This is your first weight aid. To ride on a straight line, place **equal weight on both seat bones**.

Now try to sit only on the left seat bone while continuing to push forward with the legs. In other words, put more weight on the left seat bone but remain in the saddle with both. Your left hip will lower slightly; your left knee will be in a slightly lower position. Watch that you do not collapse or bend over to one side. The best way to avoid this is "stepping" heavier into the stirrup of this side. You will feel your horse move more to the left (when the horse is not concentrating or not very sensitive to the rider's aids, he might not respond immediately). You have just used another weight aid — **putting weight on one of the seat bones**. The horse will feel your weight on one side and become a little unbalanced. Trying to rebalance himself, he will step underneath your weight by moving to the left. When he has moved as far as you had intended, re-center your weight on both seat bones.

Experiment with this on a chair first. Sit on the chair as you did when you tried out your seat bones and the muscles around them — straight, supple, no hollow back. Now move your left hip forward without using the right one. You feel a pressure change — there is more weight on your left seat bone and almost no pressure on the right one. Your left knee will tend to drop. Now try this to the right, too, to feel it. Never lean to the side so that one shoulder lowers when you shift one hip forward. Try this common mistake on the chair to feel what happens — you collapse to this side, your weight and buttocks will move to the opposite side, and you will lose the elements that should influence your horse. When riding a turn or bent line, be sure that you turn your upper body slightly in the direction of the turn, purposely moving your inside shoulder a little back, your outside slightly forward so your chest shows more toward the side of the turn. This way you automatically shift weight on the inside seat bone without the danger of collapsing to this side. This is the same way we use our upper body when walking into a turn on our own feet. Try walking straight ahead, then do some turns to the left and right. You unconsciously turn your upper body into the direction of the turn, moving your shoulders.

We use weight on one of the seat bones during all movements in which we flex or bend the horse to support the rein and leg aids. On a correctly trained advanced horse, shifting the weight to one of the seat bones is a major influencing aid.

The third weight aid, **taking all the weight off the horse's back**, is what you always perform in the forward seat. When you lean slightly forward with your upper body, your weight shifts from the buttocks to your thighs and stirrups. We use this weight aid to unburden the back and/or hindquarters of the horse during a warm-up, when starting a young horse, or when doing the rein back for the first time. Reining back the horse means we ask him to take several steps backward. We usually start this from a halt and let the horse move backward for three to four steps, or one horse length. (For more details on the rein back, see chapter 10.)

You will use the **back aid** with the weight aid, as well as with all other aids. The back aid is also called **bracing the spine.** Do some ground exercises first to experience the motion. Take a seat on the chair again, not too far back. Sit upright and keep your legs in front of you slightly spread apart. Let your hands rest on top of your knees. Now tense your back muscles so that your hips move — and the chair tips slightly. This is the correct movement for your back aid.

Try standing in front of a table that can slide easily on the floor (so close that you touch it with your body). Now try to push the table forward without using your hands or stepping forward with your feet but by bending the upper body forward or back. You will move your pelvis forward by contracting your belly and lower back muscles. This movement is your back aid. A third way to learn about the feeling of bracing the spine is the well-known swing example. Think about how it feels to sit upon a swing and make it go. This use of your muscles and pelvis to propel the swing is the same as when you give a back aid. When you use it in the saddle, the horse will feel pushed forward toward the bit. It will take awhile to learn how to perform this correctly, but once you achieve it, you will know.

Normal pelvis position

Bracing the spine

Remember what you learned in the previous chapter about sitting the trot. Let's split the horse's trot into the individual moments to see exactly what happens: The horse's back swings up and down in the trot. When the back lifts, the rider slightly contracts belly and lower back muscles. This tilts the lower pelvis forward. The next moment the horse's back lowers. The rider releases the contraction of belly and lower back muscles. The lower part of the pelvis moves back. The motion must be within the horse's rhythm of motion. This very

Hollowed back

same motion intensified for short moments (one or more steps) changes into the bracing of the spine.

Use the aid of bracing the spine with weight on either one or both seat bones. Contracting belly and lower back muscles for only a few strides at a time engages the horse to carry more weight on his hind legs and move them more forward toward his center of gravity. This is desired when doing half halts to prepare for transitions and movements so that these do not happen with too much rein aid and insufficient activity of the horse's hind legs.

It is important to brace the spine only for short moments. Continuous use will deaden the horse's response and desire to go forward. In addition, overuse will restrict the rider's ability to swing sufficiently when sitting a gait. Also avoid leaning back too far, drawing up your thighs and knees, and tensing the buttock muscles.

THE LEG AIDS

A correct leg aid varies in the leg's position, the amount of pressure it applies, and the order of pushing. The leg aids create and maintain the horse's forward motion. The forward-driving part of the leg is the lower leg, the inside of the calf. We drive the horse forward with our leg aid by giv-

ing pressure with the calf on the horse's belly. The moments we do not push we still keep the calf in contact with the horse's belly so we can feel it.

The normal **forward-driving leg** is at the girth. This means the front of the lower leg is kept right behind the back edge of the girth. Remember the vertical line that runs from shoulder to hip to heel in order to find this position.

Forward-driving leg

We accept small discrepancies in this vertical line when they result from a different anatomical shape of the horse or a different physical build of the rider. Change an incorrect saddle at once.

As the hind legs of the horse are his forward-driving power, we always want to engage them when we push. We apply pressure to the horse's belly muscles by short, strong contractions of our calf muscles, which will engage his hind legs to move forward.

Applied the moment the horse's lateral hind leg extends forward, this pressure encourages the leg's activity.

A certain amount of influence exists without active muscle work of the rider, provided that the horse has been correctly trained and has achieved enough sensitivity. As the horse's belly swings against your legs with the rhythm of motion, contact with your calves will automatically influence his hind legs.

The young horse has learned that leg pressure means to move forward. (A green horse will not move forward right away in response to your leg pressure. Careful use of a crop at the same moment will help him to understand.)

The order of using leg pressure depends on the gait we are riding. We have a different way of pushing the horse forward for each gait because the horse is using his feet in a different order in each case. In riding dressage we want to push the horse all the time, but that does not mean we always have to use a lot of strength. The amount of pressure can be minimal in some instances and released the next. The release of pressure does not mean that the leg is moving. Maintain contact by keeping the leg in place, but don't apply pressure. A rider who does not maintain lower-leg contact then suddenly pushes can disturb the rhythm of the movement. Applying the leg aid with more of a kicking motion may cause the same problem and will deaden the horse's reactions to leg aids. The same will happen if your lower leg swings back and forth while pushing. In this case you will use a lot of power that will never reach the horse.

The **sideways-pushing leg** is positioned approximately one hand's width farther back. We use it to push the horse to the side. When the lower left leg gives pressure, for example, the horse will move away to the opposite or, in this case, right side. The sideways-pushing leg influences the diagonal pair of legs to move sideways and forward.

The **guarding or supporting leg** is held in the same position as the sideways-pushing leg, one hand's width behind the girth. The guarding leg is often underused by the beginner because it is difficult to feel. We do not use it as actively as the sideways-pushing leg. It is mainly kept in passive contact with the horse's belly and only sometimes briefly used with active pressure. You will use it as the outside-leg aid in canter, when working on bent lines and in many other movements. Whenever one leg alone is used driving forward or sideways, the opposite leg has to guard the hindquarters from drifting sideways in order to keep front and hind legs on the same track.

You probably already feel that the horse tends to drift to the outside with his hind legs when riding on bent lines. That is something we do not want. We want to have the horse bent around our inside leg and aligned with the bend of the line we are riding. It is very natural for horses to like to stay straight or drift to the outside. Without pressure, they mostly will not bend. It takes a lot more concentration and work to bend. Horses are sometimes no better than we are. They take the easier way when possible.

We also want the horse straight in his longitudinal axis on straight lines or, as said before, bent on bent lines. As every horse is naturally crooked (comparable to our being left- or right-handed and therefore more stiff on one side), we have to prevent the horse from getting crooked or not bent.

When you are riding through a corner at the wall, this wall will fence the horse and prevent him from drifting to the outside or shifting his hind legs there. As soon as we leave the wall, we will not have this natural fencing on the outside. The guarding leg aid acts as a fence. The guarding or supporting leg held just in contact with the horse's body keeps the horse's hind legs where we want them.

THE REIN AIDS

The rein aids include everything you do with your reins — taking, holding, or releasing pressure. We need rein aids to ride the horse on the bit, to make him supple and sensitive to the bit, to keep his concentration, to make preparations for transitions between gaits, to stop, to back up, and to bend. Many riders forget that each rein aid needs to be given in combination with weight/back and leg aids. The hands should only provide a frame in which the horse can act, but they should never force head and neck into position. Giving rein aids, the rider has to take care that each fist stays on its side and does not move over the withers. The correct length of rein is very important. As the correct length can vary depending on what you are doing in each gait, the rider needs to shorten and lengthen the reins during training. Shortening the reins, the rider takes the rein to be shortened over into his other fist. The now-free fist opens, slides forward, and takes the rein back to the desired place.

Be careful to close the fists enough that the reins do not slide through, so you do not have to continually shorten them. This would disturb work. Also do not ride with "hard hands," which are hands closed so tight that they are stiff and fixed in one spot. A hard or shaking hand cannot feel if the horse chews on the bit and becomes supple in the poll. The shaking hand makes the horse numb on the bit because he receives uncontrolled jerks in the mouth with each shaking. You see this often when a beginner does posting trot. His hands move up and down in the way his body does.

To be a skillful and sensitive rider, you have to learn to have soft hands, to feel the horse's reaction through the reins. Before any rein action, a sensitive rider needs to feel through the bit how the horse is working at that moment. Then you should take action, applying rein aids in combination with weight and legs, doing half halts, which are described in detail later in this chapter.

I discuss the giving rein — releasing pressure on the rein — first because you should never set the other rein aids above this one. When you apply a lot of rein pressure for a particular purpose, you should release some or all of your pressure momentarily once the horse obeys. You may be astonished at the effect. It is very simple. Often the rider takes a little too much pressure or holds it too long (you start to pull on the rein instead of giving rein aids, which means take and give). When you pull, the horse will do the same. You, as the superior-thinking partner in this relationship, need to be the first one to give up the pulling contest. This doesn't mean that you let the horse win and disobey. Instead, you show the horse an easier way to relieve the pressure. In the worst case, the stronger horse will win or at least not be supple. If the horse continues to disobey, try other aids in different exercises.

Rein aids require having a contact with the horse's mouth (for the term "contact" see chapter 11). This means you take up the reins so that you have a steady connection, a little pressure on the rein. Take the reins so that they do not hang loosely, except when you intend to ride on a loose rein. This basic contact involves very little pressure. But it will vary depending on the horse and the situation.

You may feel that you have already disturbed the horse in the mouth by pulling on the reins in order to keep a contact. Never pull; just keep contact. With a short rein, the horse will be able to lean on your hands. You will lean on the horse's mouth. When you give rein aids, you are supposed to take pressure and release it again. If you do this with a loose rein, the application of pressure will be abrupt. Already having contact will require just a small amount of pressure to achieve a smooth transition. You will be able to take up and release without the reins becoming loose or slack.

Now let us explain exactly what we are doing with our hands when we give rein aids. We have established contact with the horse's mouth because we have taken up the reins.

Releasing pressure (give rein) after a taking rein aid means the fists move forward into the position we had before taking the rein. We also can just open our fists a little or move the hands slightly forward to decrease the amount of pressure on the rein. To open the fist, separate the little finger and ring finger slightly, keeping forefinger and thumb tight to maintain a grip on the rein. This can be very short and slight, following the taking rein aid.

We use the giving rein when we release the taking rein, as an offer to the horse to be softer and suppler on the bit. We give and retake for a certain number of steps to check the horse's self-carriage.

We use the giving rein when we let the horse slowly and softly take the reins through our hands and stretch in the neck. The horse is on a long rein (where we still have contact to his mouth). We use it when we give the reins completely until the horse has stretched head and neck as forward and downward as possible and

Letting the horse stretch forward-downward

the rider has no contact with his mouth. (For the terms "to give and retake the reins," "let the horse stretch forward-downward on the reins," "to give the reins completely," and "to ride on a long rein," see chapter 11.)

Stretching the hand or the whole arm forward for a few moments (to give and retake the reins) is possible if the horse will keep his head and neck position and his pace without the absolute control of the rider. Stretching the hand and the whole arm forward and then giving up the contact to the horse's mouth by letting the reins slide through the fists is possible. (*Zuegel aus der Hand kauen lassen* is the German term for "giving the reins completely" and is often used without translation in the United States.) It is a movement of its own.

The **taking rein (taking pressure)** happens on three levels. It is also called cueing the horse because you apply the taking rein to prepare the horse for something, gain his concentration, and make him softer and more submissive on the rein. The first level would be closing your fist a little more (followed by relaxing the grip again). With this you might only give a few ounces more of pressure, but that is often enough. The next, stronger level will be twisting your fist (turning it in so the little finger comes more toward your belly) and turning it out into the normal hand position again. At the strongest level, you move your whole arm back slightly to get a great amount of pressure. This level might be required when the horse ignores the other, milder cues.

Just try the two first levels before you use the third to allow the horse to react to soft aids and have more fun with sensitive and fair riding. The taking rein causes the bend to one side, gives direction for turns, changes the pace of a gait, prepares for transitions (where we can use the taking or restraining rein), and gets the horse's attention.

There is an easier way to use the taking rein to bend and turn a young horse, the **giving direction rein aid**. Instead of taking pressure backward, the rider moves the inside hand sideways in the direction of the intended turn. Using your inside hand and rein like a lungeing rein will make sense to the young horse. This way he will more promptly obey the rider's request. It is important when leading the horse with a sideways-moving hand to release pressure immediately after turning. This rein aid can also be very useful when starting to train the horse in lateral movements. It is commonly referred to as the inside opening rein.

The **maintaining** or **restraining rein** aid means holding the pressure you have for a specified moment. Use this rein aid when the horse is going against or above the bit. You can apply the maintaining rein instead of a taking rein when the horse is sufficiently submissive (for example, in half halts or the rein back). This can be the pressure you have with the mere contact to the horse's mouth or the pressure you achieve by the taking rein aid. To be able to hold the pressure, you keep the fists closed more tightly. Combined with stronger leg pressure and back aid, this should make your horse more submissive on the rein and more active in the hind legs. Try not to hold the pressure too long to keep the horse sensitive and content. We use it on horses that lean too strongly on the reins. It is important to release the pressure the moment the horse gets soft on the bit and supple in the poll.

Use the **guarding** or **supporting rein aid** on the outside rein in combination with a taking rein aid on the inside. A taking rein on the inside to flex and bend the horse, or give direction, needs support from the opposite rein. When only one rein will bend or turn the horse, he may bend overly or turn his whole neck too much, which can result in him losing his balance. In addition, the outside shoulder will not be guarded, so the horse probably follows the inside rein and bends to this side but still moves straight or to the outside.

When you ask your horse to turn, the pure bend to one side with one rein is not enough to move the horse there. You need a fence on the outside, a counter pressure that will cause the horse to follow the inside rein but not over bend to this side.

The guarding outside rein needs to release as much as the flexing and bending inside rein takes. In other words, when we use a taking rein aid on the inside, we keep slight pressure on the outside. The outside hand remains close to the horse's neck. This way we achieve only as much bend as we desire and make the horse react and turn when wanted. Normally this outside pressure is a little less than the pressure of the inside taking rein, but it can develop to a taking rein with a lot more pressure when necessary. Still, this guarding rein should be elastic in the rhythm of the horse's motion to avoid two opposing commands.

When we do not have the guarding rein as counter pressure to the taking rein, giving bend, the horse will, as we say, escape over the outside shoulder. With the guarding rein, we frame the horse's head and neck in front of the shoulders and control the outside front leg of the horse. When the guarding rein takes and keeps too much pressure, the horse is not able to follow the inside bending rein and feel comfortable within the two opposing commands. He may then tilt his head in the poll, which is incorrect. Riding bent lines, the rider's outside fist should stay as close as possible to the horse's withers so that the outside rein is in contact with the horse's neck.

HALF HALTS

The cue

In order to write this book for English-speaking riders in America, I had to study the dressage terminology. As dressage is still rather new in the United States, there is little fixed terminology for certain instances in riding.

Part of my intention with this book is to define dressage terms for the learning rider to enable instructors and students to speak the same language. When the instructor is able to use short commands and terms during a lesson instead of extensive explanations, and the student knows the longer meaning of these terms, lessons are much more efficient. The instructor does not need to waste time with longer explanations of what he wants to say. Long, intensive talks and discussions about training are a very positive and helpful addition to lessons, but they should happen after riding.

What German dressage calls *halbe parade/ganze parade* is half halt and full halt in American terminology. Another well known, but not official, word is "cueing" the horse. In my efforts to avoid creating new terms when they already exist, I have used the term half halt in this chapter, although I do not like what these words suggest to the rider. The half and near halt have nothing to do with halting. They may be very confusing for the beginner. In training sessions I prefer to use the term cue instead of half halt, but I will stick with the term half halt in this book and use cue for clarity only. In contrast with the half halt, which is a way of using the aids, the full and near halt are movements that will be explained in chapter 10. The classical system does not have a special term for the near halt. The near halt is a number of half halts given inside one gait to reduce the pace.

The half halt is a short, stronger use of rein, weight, and leg aids. The number and frequency of half halts required depends on the training level of the horse.

We use half halts for the following:
- transitions from one gait to the other
- to let the horse step through the poll
- to keep or improve the head and neck position
- to concentrate and prepare the horse for a new movement
- to collect or regulate the gait in speed
- to reach or improve collection and the raising of the forehand
- to prevent the horse from pulling or hanging on the reins.

The rider uses a taking or maintaining rein aid (he cues on the rein) while simultaneously giving weight aid on both seat bones and a forward-driving leg aid, followed by an immediately giving rein aid. The half halt is given in the rhythm of motion as often as necessary until the rider achieves his intended goal. To do correct half halts, a correct seat is necessary.

How does it feel? Weight and leg aids drive forward against a taking or maintaining rein given on one or both sides. As soon as you feel the horse responding correctly, follow with the giving rein aid. If necessary, apply the half halt a few times in a row until achieved. The forward-driving aids will give forward impulse and bring the horse more strongly against the bit. The restraint on the rein will bring the hind legs more underneath the center of gravity. The horse's reaction depends on the intensity of the half halt as well as the horse's training level and that of the horse-rider combination. When the rein aid in the half halt is not given sensitively enough, this will work backward and block the hind legs instead of letting them swing forward. If the rein aid in the half halt is only given on one side, the other rein has to maintain a soft counter pressure so that the bit is not pulled out of the mouth.

You may think of the half halt as "something you do with the reins." This is very understandable, as humans like to solve things with their hands first. Hands only is not correct; we combine all our aids to do a half halt. To know this is important because the rider accomplishes a lot with half halts. The half and the full halt are shown as exercises/movements in the classical system. You will find them in that category.

Common mistakes doing the half halt:
- not enough driving aids, too strong rein aid
- pulling on the rein without giving rein aid
- not enough maintaining rein aid, opened fists, reins too long
- falling forward with the upper body, leaning back too far
- half halts not sensitive, not firm enough.

On a talented, correct, and more highly trained horse, we will be able to get the right feeling for a good half halt because the horse will react right away and correctly. But not everybody has the opportunity to learn on a well-trained horse. It may take longer to get the feel when riding a badly trained, difficult, or unsound horse.

The beginning rider often uses too much rein — he pulls back — and for too long. Then all he feels is that he falls forward in the upper body because the horse is slowing down, putting all his weight on the front legs, probably pulling against the strong rein, and only marching on instead of reacting. On the very well-trained horse, the beginner may bring him from a canter to a halt when he only intended to come to a trot because he is used to the stronger aids needed for less trained horses. Learning to do good half halts and finding the right amount of aids and timing takes a long time for the beginner.

The whole of dressage training consists of half halts, which are given more softly and less visibly as the horse advances. We can apply the rein aid in the half halt in various ways, for which the rider needs to learn the feeling. There can be a short taking of the rein on the inside or outside only. The cues can be given periodically in a left/right/left/right manner.

ADDITIONAL AIDS

In addition to the physical instructions we can give with our body, we can use our voice, a whip, and spurs to communicate with the horse and make our wishes clear. The right thinking and breathing techniques are additional aids that actually influence the horse, as well as the rider, in body and mind.

The voice

The way we use our voice can be very important in the training of a horse, especially the young one. The voice is a way to communicate with the horse not only while riding but at all times. The language you use is not important, but your voice must have the right intonation. A word spoken in a soft, sweet, and long tone communicates a different message than when spoken in a sharp, short, aggressive tone.

The horse's hearing is extremely good — it is not necessary to yell at him to communicate. Horse people who yell a lot conceal insecurity and fright. The use of your voice in one way or another to influence the horse should not entertain or disturb other people around you. In an official dressage-show test, a rider is not allowed to talk to his horse. This policy tests each rider's ability to use body aids to influence the horse. However, a lot of riders and horses are very nervous, and I believe the use of a low voice should be allowed.

Drawing words out and using a soft, quiet intonation can gain a horse's trust and calm one that is hyperactive or afraid. Soft words are used for every down transition with hyper or young horses to help them understand the aids. Soft words may bring about more fluid transitions without over-using the reins. Using your voice softly may help teach the horse new movements (like halt or stepping backward).

Sharp, short intonation can encourage forward movement with more engagement, support a command, punish, threaten before using physical ways of influencing the horse, and increase the horse's concentration on the rider. Like words and the hissing of a crop or whip, the sound of a clicking tongue will influence the horse also. Beware of clicking the tongue too often. It is a bad habit and hard to get rid of.

Riding whips, crops

If necessary, use a whip for the following:

• To bring the young, green horse slowly to understand the forward-driving aids of the rider. The whip is used first as a forward-driving aid and simultaneously with the pushing leg aid for support.

• For more advanced horses that do not react well enough to the forward-driving leg aid.

• For increasing concentration and engaging the hindquarters.

A dressage whip should not be too short, at least 100–120 centimeters long if the horse is not afraid of it. Lighter influence is possible when holding the whip a little below the top, more at the center of gravity. Carry the whip where you can apply it to the belly behind the rider's leg. Touching the horse at the flanks can be useful, too, but some horses tend to throw their hindquarters up when touched there. We can also use it at the horse's shoulder to support sideways-driving aids or to help the beginning rider to start into the canter.

Always carry the whip on the side where you need it. In an enclosed arena, it is best inside the fist so that the whip does not touch the wall. Be careful not to disturb the horse's mouth when using the whip or moving it from one hand to the other. Try twisting the hand sideways at the wrist to touch the horse with the whip in order to not jerk on the horse's mouth.

Always use a whip with sense and sensitivity. The horse should respect it but not be afraid of it. Never use it when you are angry or upset. On a lazy horse, a short but very deliberate and precise use of the whip is more effective than a soft, constant use that brings no reaction from the horse. As the whip supports the forward-driving aids, use it in the rhythm of motion at same moment you use the driving aids. Otherwise, you might push the horse out of rhythm.

The spurs

Spurs should never substitute for the pushing leg or be used too often to punish the horse. We use spurs to give finer leg aids. The use of spurs, whip, or both together depends on the horse. Again, only the rider who already has a correct and supple seat and influence should use spurs.

The first time you try spurs, use short ones with rounded edges and no rowel. Later, choose the right one for the length of your leg, the shape of the horse's belly, and the sensitivity of the horse. We do have, for example, horses with a belly shaped wide on top and narrow below. You will have trouble reaching the belly with a spur of normal length without pulling up your heels and therefore losing the correct seat. In this case, selecting a longer spur is not to be stronger or more aggressive, but to allow you to reach the horse without twisting your leg.

You can also vary the intensity of the spur by the way you attach it to your boots. You can only use low-set spurs when drawing up the heel slightly (probably for a sensitive horse that you do not want to touch accidentally with the spur). Set as high as possible, you can use the spur without the danger of drawing up your heels all the time.

We divide the use of spurs into three levels of pressure. First, touch the horse's belly with the spurs just to let him feel it. Second, apply pressure with the spur as a more intense and firm request for the horse's attention. Third, jab with the spur to demand the horse's attention or to punish him. When the spur is used to punish the horse, the rider must be very sure of what he is doing, as it may spoil the trust between horse and rider, as every kind of incorrect, emotional punishment can do.

Use whip and spur briefly but precisely to keep the horse sensitive. Used too much and often, they will deaden the horse. I prefer to use spurs rather than a whip when the horse is able to respond calmly to them. The horse often can understand the relationship from leg aid to spur better than leg aid to whip. In addition, many horses overreact to the whip by tensing.

THINKING AND BREATHING TECHNIQUES

The thinking technique is a very helpful aid to influence and relax the horse's, as well as the rider's, mind and body. I have mentioned before that the adult rider often prevents himself from learning more quickly and easily because he thinks too much. This means the rider tries to ride by letting the brain manage the body actions. This way all action stays mechanical and often tense, and the real harmony between rider and horse cannot be reached.

Using thinking as a technique to ride the horse means we want to control and command all our body actions with the brain. For example, in the beginning we surely have to think actively how to do a posting trot, how and when to move up and down, how to hold parts of our body, which muscles to contract or loosen. At a later stage, we perform this exercise so automatically that it is unconscious. Then we will have time to use our brain for other, important things. So you first use your brain to learn the technical and mechanical part of riding, then you perform the seat more unconsciously and use the aids with feeling, leaving the brain free to be aware.

At some point, you may encounter a horse that overreacts to your aids. He almost explodes when you start a canter. He panics in response to your body aids. Try to "think" the canter depart instead of actually applying much of a physical aid. Just by thinking your body will already start enough action to tell the sensitive horse what you want him to do. Another horse may jig into a trot repeatedly when he is supposed to walk. Think the walk motion while also breathing deep and slow, so the horse can sense your evenness and relaxation.

Listen with your body every day to how your horse feels so you can choose the right kind of work. Become aware of stiffness and tension in your body so you can release them. Learn to become aware of yourself and your horse instead of trying to capture everything with logic.

Breathing usually is something we do without actually thinking about it. Yet when afraid, nervous, or tense, our breathing rhythm — and the horse's — changes. We may hold our breath when concentrating or nervous, breathe fast and irregularly in difficult situations, or breathe convulsively when something is creating tension. Hold your breath for a moment, then return to normal breathing. You will feel your body tense while you are holding your breath.

This tension in our body is absorbed by the horse, which will tense and stiffen. His senses tell him that something has changed, and he may anticipate a frightening situation. Sometimes your horse may see a "ghost" and spook because you were afraid of something and held your breath. Horses sense your mental status by your physical reactions. They immediately sense changes in our body and mind.

If you are aware that you are not relaxed and breathing deeply take a few moments to breath in and out deeply and slowly. When you feel your horse tense because something makes him nervous or afraid, breathe very consciously, even with a loud sigh in between breaths, to let your horse feel that you are not worried. Try talking softly to the horse. When you are talking, you aren't able to hold your breath.

7 | How to Structure a Riding Session

To train a horse successfully in dressage, we structure each riding session using a progression of movements and figures. You need to learn and understand this structure so you and your horse can progress efficiently and happily. Each training session consists of a **warm-up phase** (preparation for work, achievement of suppleness), a **working phase** (improvement of former exercises, starting new movements or paces), and a **relaxation phase** (check of work, relaxation of body and mind).

THE WARM-UP PHASE

Every athlete needs to prepare his body before training and competing in order to perform at his best and not risk injury. This also applies to the horse. In dressage, a warm-up prepares and relaxes the horse physically and mentally. Training with no warm-up or an insufficient warm-up can create health problems such as joint damage, sprained or torn muscles, or increased tension of body or mind, which will prevent a productive session. The warm-up may differ depending on the level the horse has reached, his temperament, and whether he is kept in a stall, paddock, or large pasture.

During the warm-up phase, we loosen the horse's muscles, tendons, and ligaments. As they warm up, blood circulation increases.

The exercises of the warm-up phase also serve as warm-up work for the rider. In addition, you can do some stretching and warm-up exercises on the ground before starting to ride.

Warm-up work should last ten to twenty minutes. The amount of time, order, and kind of gaits and movements vary depending on the training level, temperament, and character of each horse. In preparation for work, we want to make the nervous horse calm and the lazy one eager. Advanced horses often need only a brief warm-up, as they become supple more readily. Young horses need a longer warm-up — it is the main part of a training session for them.

Before the warm-up begins, we walk the horse on a loose or long rein for at least ten minutes. The joint fluids need this much time to increase temperature and elasticity, and to work without risk of injury. A very good way to relax the horse is to take a short trail ride. This phase of walking should also always be done before we lunge or free jump the horse.

In lower training stages, never ride the walk on the bit for very long. The horse is not yet submissive enough to feel unrestricted and do the walk freely. The walk could develop problems if you try to force a young horse to walk on the bit. If there is a need to train the walk, ride the horse on a loose rein and go for trail rides to improve his walk without interfering with the reins.

Always precede any cantering with some working trot in your warm-up because the trot is easier on joints and tendons even when the horse supples better at a canter. Ride posting trot on wide lines, such as going large 20-meter circles and serpentines with wide loops, until the horse accepts a steady contact on the reins and supples.

If your horse is difficult to warm up at the rising trot, try starting him in the sitting trot at a slightly calmer pace. For this you have to be able to sit very smoothly. Begin posting only when the horse is on the aids and supple. Choosing the right amount of forwardness of the trot is also important. If you rush the horse forward, you may increase his tension; however, if you permit your horse to trot in a slow, lazy manner, his hind legs will not be fully engaged and he may not connect on the rein.

Change rein often to help the horse stretch evenly on both sides, changing on the full or short diagonal or over the centerline. Do not yet ride changing figures, which contain small turns. Figures containing turns 10 meters or smaller belong in the working phase. The horse needs to be warmed up sufficiently to do them correctly and without harm.

Following the trot work, ask the horse to make repeated transitions from trot to working canter and back on easy lines and circles. These changes are especially valuable to supple and strengthen a horse's back muscles. Decide which of the two gaits is more relaxing for your horse and take advantage of that gait.

Horses that are very difficult to supple warm up best with lots of extended canter and riding over cavaletti. Canter is often the most efficient way to supple a horse's back muscles if the horse remains calm and content.

Select those exercises that are effective for the type of horse you ride. With lazy horses ride lots of trot-canter transitions and extensions in trot and canter to make them more eager and attentive. Long phases in the same gait and pace might slow down lazy horses even more. For nervous horses with a tendency to rush, we stay in the same gait longer, doing more work on bend lines such as serpentines and leaving extensions until the working phase. Many transitions in a row during warm-up would make sensitive horses eventually more hyper. Find out if your horse supples better with more trot or more canter work.

You also may include some of the following movements in the warm-up:

- Riding single loops and serpentines with three to four loops
- Lengthening of stride or slight extensions in trot and canter
- Transitions from walk to trot, trot to walk
- Frequent changes of lead
- Turn on the forehand
- Trotting and cantering over cavaletti, varying setup and distances
- Leg-yielding in different variations (with the more advanced horse)

Additional possibilities that work well for some horses are lungeing, trail riding, small jumps, in-and-outs, and free jumping.

You may choose to canter a young or extremely sensitive horse in the forward seat instead of the dressage seat.

Once a horse is accustomed to lateral movements or leg-yielding, they work well to supple the horse and make him attentive and obedient to the aids.

How do you know when the horse is warmed up?

The horse is warmed up when he stays on the aids easily, moving forward freely and willingly without hesitation or tensed muscles. The horse now waits for the rider's driving aids. He chews softly on the bit with a closed mouth without grinding his teeth or biting on the bit. His paces are rhythmic and even. His tail is carried slightly higher and straight and swings rhythmically. He will occasionally snort, which is a sign of suppled muscles and free breathing. The rider can sit comfortably because the horse's back is swinging. The horse stretches forward-downward into the bit and is submissive. He has a relaxed and contented expression.

The absolute test for suppleness and submissiveness is the movement *Zuegel aus der Hand kauen lassen* — letting the horse gradually take the reins out of your hands — which tells us if the horse is swinging his back and ready to stretch his muscles. It is frequently done during the warm-up phase but also during the subsequent work and relaxation phases. We do it most often at the trot but also at the walk or canter. It will always be a reward for the horse because it allows him to stretch his neck muscles for a moment. The same checkpoint for the quality and effectiveness of training is the movement *Ueberstreichen* — give and retake the reins (extending one or both hands forward for a few steps). These movements confirm if you have achieved suppleness, submissiveness, and self-carriage. (For both terms see chapter 11.)

What we can do wrong during warm-up

A proper warm-up should increase the horse's capability for performance. If the horse is not relaxed and supple in the working phase, your warm-up may not have been long enough or it may have been too long so that your horse is already tired. Warm-ups can also fail when the rider uses the wrong movements or does one for too long and doesn't offer the horse enough breaks. Incorrect movements can include very small turns, sitting trot too early, any collecting movement when the horse is not physically warmed up yet, any movement or figure the horse cannot perform very well yet, or any exercise that makes the horse nervous during warm-up. Overuse of an exercise can tire the horse, while too much stretching and relaxing will fail to produce engagement in the horse. Overuse of the rein — the rider tries to shape the horse with the rein aids only — can negate the benefits of the warm-up as well.

Depending on the individual horse, we may have to change the order of learning when we find a different way works better. The training concept, especially for canter and lateral movements, can vary much with individual horses.

THE WORKING PHASE

The purpose of the working phase is to improve movements the horse already knows and introduce new ones. The kind of movements, the pace of gaits, and the school figures depend on the horse's and rider's training level. The amount of time depends on the horse's condition and his capacity to concentrate. When teaching the horse new figures, transitions, or movements, keep in mind that they will never be perfect right away. Only with constant and patient training and repetition will you achieve perfection.

Perfection can be the absolutely correct and good-looking performance judged by theoretical and idealistic standards. Sometimes just parts of a test or training session can be perfect — perfect enough for a sport in which two individuals work together.

Isn't it perfect when a not-so-great rider and a not-so-great horse finally have moments in their work that come close to the theoretic ideal?

If a moment, movement, gait, or transition "feels" perfect because the rider and horse work in unison, it is perfect.

If your horse responds with tension or resistance during the working phase, quickly go back to some of the suppling movements of the warm-up phase and use the *Zuegel aus der Hand kauen lassen* as a gauge of your work. We also break up the working phase with brief periods during which we ride on a loose rein to let the horse recover physically and mentally.

Work in new movements step by step. If you feel that the horse has gained a slight understanding of what you are asking, be satisfied. Reward your horse to let him know that he is on the right track. Quit this movement for the day and work at it again during the next training session.

You may want to end the daily session when the horse does something really good. This way your horse will remember the positive feeling and the reward when you resume work. He will be eager to work for you. If you work on a movement at the end of a session and he becomes tense, nervous, or resistant, don't end the lesson at this point. Do a relaxing and well-known exercise to finish the day's working phase. Rewarding the horse during work and ending on a positive note are both very important training tools.

Up to first level, start training the following movements:

• Free and medium walk on a long or loose rein to avoid influencing the gait.

• Working trot, riding loops, serpentines, and 20-meter circles. Slowly decrease the circles to 10-meter voltes. Ride most of the working phase trot in sitting trot. Use the bent lines to improve flexion and bend in the horse. The horse must adapt to the bend in his longitudinal axis. The legs of the forehand and hindquarters must be in the same track.

• Change rein often to work both sides of the horse evenly. Frequent changes of direction give you the opportunity to improve the horse's submissiveness and reaction to changing flexion and bend from side to side.

• Transitions from the walk to the trot and back, halts from the walk or trot. As transitions require lots of half halts, they are the best way to increase submissiveness. All transitions must be clear but not abrupt, and soft and elastic. If some of the halts are not square yet, do not correct too much. This may make the horse nervous and cause him to shift around continuously. Do one step at a time, and be content with immobility for a while.

A correct square halt should result from a correctly ridden transition into the halt and not by correctional aids. The more submissively the horse does the transition, the more apt the horse will be to stand in a square halt right away.

• Working canter on the true lead, going large and riding 20-meter circles.

• Transitions from the trot to the canter and back, and some transitions from the walk to the canter and back. Work to the point at which you can pick up a canter at any place in the arena. Trot/canter transitions are helpful to strengthen the horse, loosen his back muscles, and create impulsion. Walk/canter transitions increase submissiveness, obedience, and collection. Take your time training the down transition canter to walk. Let the horse move into walk with a few trot steps and by giving a lot of voice support rather than by merely pulling roughly back to the walk.

• Lengthen stride in trot and canter toward the medium pace. When trotting, do both sitting and posting in the extensions. Ask only as much at a time as possible to keep the rhythm intact and to reach a true lengthening as opposed to a faster, rushed gait. If the extended trot improves, it is a sign of the correctness of all work.

• Turns on the forehand.

• Leg-yielding at the walk and the trot. Introduce this movement to the horse at the walk. Work it at the trot after you have reached a clear understanding at the walk. After the horse is well accustomed to leg-yields, do it on various lines to make sure the horse reacts obediently whenever you ask.

• Ride some of the training time during the working phase on and from the second track, which is the line inside the first track next to the outside wall. This trains the rider to use his outside aids sufficiently and keep the horse framed between inside and outside aids. It trains the horse not to want to "lean" onto the arena walls and drift there with the outside shoulder but to listen to and accept the rider's outside aids. Advanced horses can be worked on the second track during the warm-up phase.

• Repeat the relaxing and controlling movements such as *Zuegel aus der Hand kauen lassen* (gradually letting the horse take the reins out of your hands) and *Ueberstreichen* (give and retake the reins) several times during the working phase. Many of the dressage-show tests demand these movements so you need to be able to perform them any time. Besides being control movements, they also feel rewarding to the horse. For example, the *Zuegel aus der Hand kauen lassen* allows the horse to stretch his muscles.

Usually we introduce lateral work in the walk first because the horse can organize himself easier. Sometimes you encounter horses that resist the rider very aggressively and completely when trying laterals in the walk. In this case, try starting the lateral work in the trot, where the moment of suspension, impulsion, and the higher speed usually help the process. Ride along the long side and counterflex the horse (flex him toward the arena wall). Once the horse obeys this exercise, start using the sideways-driving leg in addition (the leg showing to the outside of the arena). Always emphasize that impulsion and forwardness are maintained.

Once you have established the basic movements, proceed with the advanced movements of the second and upper levels. Here, the actual work of straightening the horse, increasing impulsion, and developing collection begins. The following movements and exercises will help your horse carry more weight on his hindquarters, which is necessary to develop collection:

• Riding medium and free walk, shortening strides toward collected walk, as well as lengthening toward extended walk. All paces above medium walk can and should be ridden with a slightly longer rein to give the horse the optimum freedom to develop the pace. Ride collected and free walk only when the horse is completely supple, submissive, and in absolute rhythm.

• Walk pirouettes from the walk or the halt. During introductory training, ride them letting the hind legs move on a much larger half circle than the final movement requires. This prevents the hind legs from becoming immobile and pivoting on the spot. If the inside hind leg pivots on the spot, we lose the gymnasticizing effect of it taking more weight. The first goal is that the horse accepts being led around. The flexion need not be correct yet.

• Reining back. If the horse is resistant or nervous about this movement, start the reining back from a turn on the forehand. Try giving all your aids to begin a turn on the forehand. When the horse starts moving, use slightly more rein pressure to achieve a few steps backward. Another possibility is doing the rein back from the ground, using a whip and your voice. Be satisfied with only one or two steps in the beginning. Always check if the diagonal pair of legs is stepping back simultaneously.

• Ride the working, collected, medium, and extended trot. Develop all paces out of the working trot by riding transitions and near halts. Always do an extension after a period of collected work to re-establish impulsion and forwardness. Transitions from collected to medium trot and reverse are of especially great gymnasticizing value. You can transfer the impulsion of a medium trot into collection and the cadence of collected trot into the extension. Only when those transitions are well established should you start the extended trot.

• Ride working, collected, medium, and extended canter. Change rein with simple changes through the walk (canter/three to four steps of walk/canter). If the horse still gets crooked, ride canter with a slight shoulder-in or counter canter on the first track to straighten the horse.

• Ride serpentines with smaller loops and voltes down to 8 meters and 6 meters in trot and canter.

• Transitions through all gaits, full halts from all gaits.

• Counter canter. Work the counter canter first while going large, keeping the corners cut flat. Later on, ride it on various lines like circles and serpentines.

• Half-pass, shoulder-in, travers. Train them at the trot first, later at the canter. Lateral movements are the rider's most valuable gymnasticizing tools. You can develop all by riding a leg-yield on the appropriate line, then changing flexion and bend during the motion. Ride combinations like shoulder-in for half of a long side, a volte at the middle, then travers for the rest of the long side or the reverse combination. This is an excellent way to improve submissiveness and obedience. Introduce half-pass zigzags when the horse becomes absolutely submissive.

• Start single flying changes and develop large canter pirouettes. Start flying changes when you have securely established the collected canter and counter canter.

Once the horse performs these movements confidently, he will be ready for high-level movements such as flying changes in a series with a certain number of canter strides in between, canter pirouettes, passage, and piaffe.

Plan your daily and weekly training sessions. Have a time frame for warm-up and working phase, allowing enough time for working on new movements in the working phase. Set goals for several weeks or months depending on your training abilities and your horse's potential. Take a moment every day during riding to concentrate on your seat and aids. This is especially important when you ride without a trainer's regular advice and correction.

Regularly use some of your training time to concentrate on figure riding. The challenge is to ride the figures correctly in different gaits. Check for perfect straightness or correct flexion and bend (depending on which is necessary in the moment), a regular pace, and a correct frame of the horse. Do various combinations of figures in a row to see how precisely you are able to ride them. This is helpful in preparing you for the next dressage test or show. In addition to figure riding, ride the dressage test for your level once in a while. Do this even when you do not intend to use your dressage training for show riding. Riding combinations of all the movements and paces that you have practiced separately will show if your horse is submissive, supple, and obedient enough to perform familiar exercises in different patterns.

Occasionally participating in a group lesson to ride in formation is good for horse and rider. The instructor will have one rider in front leading a row of several riders. Each rider is expected to follow the rider in front of him at a distance of about two horse lengths. The group performs commands given for figures or movements. Riding in formation challenges each rider to control his horse so well that he can maintain correct distance, gait, and pace in a group. It trains rider and horse to be adaptable. It is also an opportunity to work with other riders, which is especially positive for children.

Sometimes the horse makes a mistake or does not progress with a certain movement because the rider is not working correctly. Be critical about your work and admit your mistakes. Do not let anger or frustration influence your work. The more you analyze and criticize your own work, the faster training will progress.

THE RELAXATION PHASE

After you have accomplished your training goals, it is important to finish the session with a brief, relaxing work that leaves the horse with a positive memory of the training session. Horses have very good memories, and they will start more willingly and contentedly the next day when the last workout ended with a positive experience. You always start out training with easy exercises and end with a good performance. If the last exercise you attempt fails, do not do it over and over again. Go back to a simpler one and try the new one again the next time. Finishing the daily work with the *Zuegel aus der Hand kauen lassen* will give you a final check if your work was positive and successful and will release the horse from work with a good feeling while he is stretching. At the very end, walk on a loose rein to cool down the horse.

CAVALETTI TRAINING

Cavaletti training might sound like an excursion into jumping, but it enriches every kind of training, including dressage.

Cavaletti are wooden or plastic poles about two to three meters long resting on stands that can be set up at various heights. You can also use simple poles to ride over, but they may roll away when the horse steps on them and cause injuries.

It is very important to have the right distance between the cavaletti when you want to have the horse go over several in a row. Wrongly placed cavaletti will result in the opposite of our intentions. The horse will be unable to move over them in the desired manner and may even get hurt. He may lose rhythm and become tense and anxious or disobedient.

The correct distance between them depends on the gait in which you intend to ride over them. Every gait has a different length of stride. The medium distance for the walk is 0.80 meters (about 32 inches), for the trot 1.30 meters (about 51 inches), for the canter 3 meters (about 118 inches). These are the average lengths of a horse's stride in those gaits. Vary those

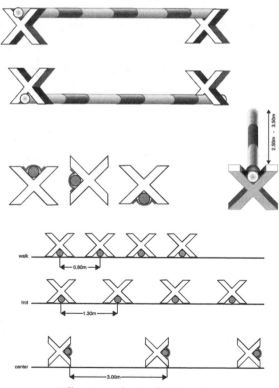

Different cavaletti and their options

distances if the horse differs from average in size and stride. For example, set up the cavaletti with shorter distances for ponies. For a tall horse with exceptionally long strides, increase the distance.

Another reason to alter the distance between cavaletti is to achieve various results. Increase the distance to encourage the horse to move with longer steps to add extension to the gait or to stretch better. Decrease the distance to collect the horse and gather his attention.

Why is cavaletti work positive for the dressage horse?

Dressage is gymnastics with which we intend to supple, strengthen, and develop the horse's muscles and joints. Cavaletti work is an excellent tool for this. Stepping over cavaletti encourages the horse to move differently, lift his feet higher, and adjust his length of stride to the distance the cavaletti are set. This works positively on joints and muscles while keeping the horse in a controlled motion. Cavaletti work helps supple muscles and gets rid of stiffness (for example, in mistrained horses). It is especially helpful in strengthening the horse's back muscles. The horse learns to balance correctly with the rider's weight. He achieves more security in his steps and learns to adjust his center of gravity quickly when necessary. You can improve the quality of walk and trot, giving both gaits more rhythm, evenness, impulsion, and expression.

For dressage horses, we use cavaletti work in walk and trot. Cantering over cavaletti does not have much value because the kind of canter stride wanted in dressage and the one over cavaletti are different. The dressage horse is supposed to canter with his forehand moving upward and the bending haunches lowering the hindquarters. Cantering over cavaletti means the horse is jumping, and here the hindquarters are moving upward, not down.

For cavaletti to be useful, the workout should not last too long. This can overstrain the muscles, resulting in atrophy (developing less) instead of developing more. The length of time used for cavaletti work varies with the horse's age, condition, training stage, and concentration span. During a training session, the work over cavaletti should not last longer than twenty minutes overall, doing a warm-up before and some more training without cavaletti after.

Cavaletti also challenge the rider's position and balance and help keep training more interesting and satisfying. You can increase your overall balance on the horse and develop more feeling for the horse's swinging back. Besides, you must learn and use the forward seat, which a dressage rider must know. You will achieve more elasticity in your seat, which will become more independent from the horse's motion.

How to use cavaletti work

You can work the horse over cavaletti by letting him move freely in the arena, by lungeing, or by riding him. You can place cavaletti in different locations in the arena and vary the number in a row, the distance between them, and their height.

We can set up cavaletti in different places in the arena on straight and on bent lines. Set up jumping wings at the sides for working the horse over cavaletti freely, on the lunge line, or for young horses or riders. Protecting the horse's legs with bandages or splint boots is a good idea.

In preparation for cavaletti work, warm up the horse for at least five to fifteen minutes. Like every other kind of training, quit cavaletti training for the day when the horse has done really well.

When the horse does cavaletti for the very first time, start with walking over a single cavaletti in the lowest position, then increase the number of cavaletti to no more than four in a row. After you have established walking over cavaletti, move onto trot work, starting with a single cavaletti again.

Free cavaletti work

Let the horse move freely in the arena, without a rider or lunge line. Often horses like this workout as much as some enjoy free jumping. As you prepare to use cavaletti, let the horse first move around without them to warm up and spend excess energy. Place the cavaletti on one of the arena's long sides. Set up wings toward the inside (like you do for a jumping lane). You can work the horse in this exercise with or without side reins. When using side reins to keep the horse on the bit and straight, be sure that he is used to moving over cavaletti without trying to jump them. Otherwise the side reins will hurt him. If you use side reins during your free work, attach them evenly on both sides.

Cavaletti work on the lunge line

To work the horse over cavaletti on the lunge line, place the cavaletti on the circle's bent line. This exercise also can be done with or without side reins. If you use them, keep the inside rein shorter to give the horse a flexion and bend to the inside. Change leads often to work the horse evenly and prevent overstraining on one side. A less experienced person should only use cavaletti with a block stand for lungeing. Lungeing a horse over cavaletti that have cross stands can be dangerous. The lunge line can get trapped when hanging down too loosely.

Riding over cavaletti at the walk

Start riding a horse over cavaletti in walk first, as this gait gives you the best control. Keep the cavaletti at a distance of 0.80m–1.10m (about 32–43 inches), with only one cavaletti in the lowest position for the beginning. Then add one at a time to no more than four in a row. Approaching the cavaletti, the rider leans slightly forward in the upper body so he will not lose balance if the horse jumps suddenly. Walk cavaletti with a long or loose rein, which improves the clarity of the four beats of the walk. Walking over cavaletti will especially help horses that tend to pace or jig. Vary the distances to work on the different paces of the gait; ride the collected walk on the bit and the extended walk with a loose rein.

Riding over cavaletti in trot

After your horse is comfortable walking over cavaletti, practice trotting over cavaletti set first on straight lines, then on bent lines. Set the cavaletti at distances of 1.30m–1.50m (about 51–59 inches), and adjust your stirrups two to three holes shorter.

Post the trot as you approach and keep a steady pace, with your hands set low on both sides of the withers. When your horse remains steady and calm, try riding toward the cavaletti in sitting trot. Use the forward seat over the cavaletti and give with the reins slightly to allow the horse to stretch forward-downward. Do a sitting trot over cavaletti only when the horse is absolutely accustomed to the work and the rider is able to sit the trot smoothly.

The best exercise to relax and strengthen the horse's back muscles is trotting over cavaletti while letting the horse stretch forward-downward on the reins. This exercise works especially well with horses that are difficult to ride on the bit — either horses trained incorrectly or those with natural problems in the head/neck set.

Vary your practice with shorter distances between cavaletti for work on collected paces and longer distances for extended paces. Always approach the cavaletti in the pace for which they have been set up.

8 | Training the Green Horse/ The Scale of Training

THE UNBROKEN/GREEN HORSE

Training a green horse is very different from training an older horse and should always be handled by an advanced and experienced rider. It is an extensive subject, but I will only discuss it briefly in this book.

Training horses under saddle should not start until they are at least three years old. Before then keep all work short and easy. Do not forget that depending on breed, gender, and individual development, a horse doesn't reach maturity until he is usually six or seven years old. Basic training of a green horse will provide a solid foundation of gymnastics, obedience, and education that can support any discipline that suits the horse. During basic training we can assess the horse's possibilities for a later specialization. At the end of basic training, which takes about a year, we should be able to handle the young horse in every environment. He must know and obey all rider's aids and have gained condition, elasticity, strength, and trust. The horse should be able to do dressage at about first level, jump up to two or three feet, and be familiar with trail riding. It is important for the horse's health and mental stability to increase the length and demands of his daily training slowly and steadily. The pace should be dictated by the condition and conformation of the young horse.

Balancing the young horse is the first goal. It is the basis for all future work. Basic training begins with general ground work and handling the horse in different situations and environments. We walk the horse in hand a lot, emphasizing that the young horse stay beside us all the time, not running forward or away or refusing to come with us. Leading the horse, we want to be even with his shoulder. This way we can see the horse's reactions and also easily use a crop in our left hand to tap it behind to move him forward more. Work on leading the horse on different lines, in various environments, making him stop and proceed in between to check his understanding of the cues and obedience. The horse must follow the commands easily without evading the leader or disrespecting human dominance by bumping into us.

The initial introduction to the saddle should happen when the horse feels secure but also where there is enough space to protect the horse and handler. The first day or two just lay the saddle on the horse's back without a girth. Then tighten the girth only so much that the saddle sits securely and won't move. An overly tight girth may cause a claustrophobic reaction — a blow up, rearing, bucking, or throwing himself to the ground — in the young horse. Take several days to tighten the girth fully. Lead the horse with bridle and saddle for several days before you start lungeing. You will eventually lead and lunge the horse with stirrups down, as this accustoms the horse to the later movement of the leg at his side. If the horse reacts sensitively to the bit in the mouth, lead with a rope or rein attached to the noseband only (the lateral rings of a dropped noseband work well here) or to a lungeing cavesson or halter put on top of the bridle.

The next step is lungeing the horse in preparation for riding. If necessary, have a second person lead the horse to help him understand what is being asked of him. If available, use a round pen to start lungeing. The fence and shape make it much easier to control and teach the horse. At this stage, we teach the horse driving and restraining aids using the lunge line, lungeing whip, and voice. We lunge the horse for several weeks before we start mounting. Each lungeing session should not exceed fifteen to twenty minutes. This work frame is short enough not to demand too much physically, and it also fits the green horse's attention span, which about equals that of small children. After one to two weeks we use side reins to accustom the young horse to contact on the bit. Keep the side reins extremely long the first few times, as the green horse may react with fright. We lunge at the walk and trot, introducing canter no sooner than the second week of lungeing. When the horse stretches forward into contact with the side reins and moves relaxed in all gaits, we have reached the goal of lungeing work.

The first time you mount a green horse, have an assistant lift you up.

Lie on the horse's back with your legs to the horse's left side, your upper body on the saddle, and your head toward the right so you could easily slide off the horse if necessary. Have the assistant lead you around. Next, take an upright seat, still being led. If the horse seems comfortable, ride him on the lunge line for several days before riding freely or until you establish some control. With our voice and the riding crop, used mainly at the horse's shoulder, we accustom the horse to our aids. We do only walk and trot work initially. Always post the trot to give the horse time to get accustomed to our weight. We keep our hands set very low, having only slight contact. Except for an opening leading rein, for which we move the inside hand in the direction of the turn, we do not give rein aids yet. The rider's whole intention is to follow the horse's motions elastically and passively. Voice and crop control pace and speed. During the initial period of riding, we do not work for more than fifteen to twenty minutes. We break up trot and canter work with frequent periods of walk on a loose rein to let the young horse relax and recover.

In keeping with the scale of training described later, we concentrate on rhythm and suppleness after starting to ride the horse. It is very important to give the horse enough time to react and learn. Have the patience to wait and continue the aids for several moments until the young horse understands and follows the command. Green horses still need a longer time to organize themselves and react to the rider's command. Ride only wide, large lines in all gaits, meaning no turns and bend lines below 10 meters in diameter. Anything smaller will be too physically demanding on the young horse.

Do not forget: When we start riding a green horse, our body weight disturbs his natural balance. During the initial weeks of riding the young horse, the emphasis is on letting the horse regain that balance. The young horse has to learn to adjust to the rider's weight on his back. We distinguish between the lateral balance (horizontal balance) and the balance between front and back (vertical balance). Lateral imbalances show when the young horse sways sideways in motion. A vertical imbalance shows in down transitions, during which the horse is heavy on his forehand and pulls on the reins to find support. Common signs of imbalance are pulling on the reins, hurrying, or the opposite, failure to go forward. Balancing the young horse is the first goal we need to reach. It is the basis for all future work.

Walk

Ride the walk for ten to fifteen minutes to start each training session. Also have extensive walk periods during trot and canter work to give the horse time to relax. During the first months mainly ride the walk on a loose rein to avoid disturbing the horse's rhythm, length of stride, or suppleness. We do not ride the young horse on the bit but on a long rein (for this term see chapter 11). Forward-backward following hands must allow the natural up and down nodding of the horse's head. To teach the young horse sensitive reaction to the leg aids, we use a crop when the horse is lazy instead of any squeezing or kicking with the leg. If the horse is oversensitive to leg pressure, be careful to avoid too much sudden contact with his belly for a while. A quietly supporting calf will calm the nervous horse faster because it feels steadier. The calf kept away from the horse's side will always feel sudden when used and therefore increases nervousness.

Trot

We mainly work the young horse on straight and large bend lines such as 20-meter circles. Do not train small turns and voltes yet. The young horse is physically unable to do smaller bend lines correctly or safely. The first weeks or months we only do posting trot. This does not burden the horse's back, and he will use his still-weak back muscles better. Work on establishing balance, rhythm, suppleness, and contact, and teach the horse the rider's forward-driving aids. The rider's hands keep contact with the horse's mouth, riding him on the bit but in a longer and lower frame than the advanced horse. When the hindquarters achieve driving power and rhythm and contact are secured, we start lengthening the strides for short distances. If the horse is stronger and secure on the aids, we do sitting trot for short periods, always interrupted by posting trot to avoid tiring or tensing.

Canter

Before starting any canter, we work the young horse in walk and trot

until he has gained enough balance and is easy to control and turn on circles. If he has not established his balance, you will feel this most obvious-
ly when trying to canter. The still-unbalanced horse will either try to avoid
cantering or speed up. Whenever the horse offers to canter, take the
chance and ride it. Some young horses are able to perform a canter at a
very early stage of training. They can rebalance quickly. Others will not feel
secure and comfortable with the canter for a long time. These horses may
be naturally very unbalanced or still struggling to regain their balance with
the rider. Work these young horses at a trot for a longer period before trying to canter so they can find their balance and gain confidence.

We pick up the canter coming from the arena's long side into the corner (cut the corner to make it flat). Another possibility is on a 20-meter
circle coming toward the enclosed side. Give your canter aids from the
posting trot or forward seat. Only later do we start a canter from the sitting trot. A good way to introduce canter work is giving the canter aid from
a posting trot on the "wrong diagonal" (described in chapter 5). We push
the horse forward more energetically, with the inside leg initiating the canter and the outside leg guarding. We support the leg aid by the use of the
riding crop. A slight flexion to the outside during the first work periods can
rebalance the young horse so that he will pick up the correct canter more
easily (very often helpful for the right-lead canter). If the horse becomes
faster and hurried instead of switching into a canter, establish a calm working trot first before trying again. Never punish the young horse for making
a mistake learning to canter. This will only tense and maybe scare the horse
and lead to more mistakes or open resistance.

The majority of young horses feel more comfortable with the left-lead
canter than the right. Use this to your advantage. Try the first-ever canter
and the first in each daily session on the left lead to avoid tension, resistance, or misunderstandings.

During the initial training phases we ride canter in the forward seat.
Later we switch more and more to the dressage seat, doing this change
very smoothly and only temporarily. First we do short canter periods; only

as much as the horse offers. Doing many transitions from trot to canter and back in later stages will increase elasticity, suppleness, and submissiveness and is the best way to strengthen the horse's back muscles. When the canter is well established, we start lengthening the strides to strengthen the hind legs.

It is very important for the physical and mental well being of the young horse to tailor each training session to the horse's current capacity. We spend the major part of each training session in the warm-up phase, while the demands in the working phase should increase only slowly. Keep every new exercise short. If the young horse only slightly understands and reacts to your aids, reward him immediately. Quit and ride a suppling movement that restores impulsion.

As mentioned before, we should take at least one year to do the basic training. The horse then is at about first level. This implies the horse has the training of first level and can lengthen stride at the trot and canter, leg-yield, and execute serpentines and 10-meter circles at the trot. He may not be ready to compete at this level. Compete at first level when the horse knows second. So after basic training, you want to compete the horse in training level.

The following goals are established with basic training: The horse performs all gaits in balance, with suppleness, and in rhythm. He is continuously on the bit, having a natural forwardness without hurrying. The supple horse is clearly submissive in all transitions. Bending work and immobile halts are started. The horse reacts obediently to the forward- and sideways-driving leg.

The training concept, especially for canter and lateral movements, can vary greatly with different horses. These are only two examples in which the order or kind of learning can change. You will find horses that supple up best when they are warmed up with a lot of canter. Others are naturally very unbalanced in the canter and therefore get nervous and tense when we introduce the canter at an early training stage or when canter work is done too early during a daily training session.

Usually we introduce lateral work to a horse in walk, because the horse can organize himself easier in this slow gait. Once in a while you find horses that resist the rider completely when trying lateral walk work. Here you try starting lateral work in the trot, counter flexing on the long side only at first. Once you establish this exercise, start using the sideways-driving leg as well, always emphasizing that impulsion and forwardness are kept. The moment of suspension and greater speed of the trot help to make the horse obey and understand easier.

THE SCALE OF TRAINING

Dressage is not the only way to obedience, lightness, invisible aids, and understanding, but it is definitely one that works. The rider needs submissiveness of the horse to reach all the goals of the scale of training.

Submissiveness/Durchlaessigkeit

This is the horse's willingness to follow the rider's aids while being supple, obedient, and without resistance or hesitation equally in each direction. The horse should react to and accept the forward-driving aids with greater activity of the hind legs and let his body follow the restraining rein aids without blocking them somewhere in his body.

Continuous gymnasticizing to reach the goals of the scale of training improves submissiveness, which is the measurement for correct training. The submissive horse gains rhythm in all gaits. He transmits restraining rein aids through to his hind legs. The hind legs move forward with suffi-

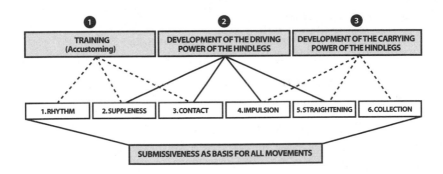

cient impulsion. The horse reacts to commands equally on both sides of his body. The rider is able to ride the submissive horse precisely the way he wants and at the desired speed.

The systematic structure for classical dressage training is called the scale of training. It consists of six elements in three phases. The elements — rhythm/balance (*Takt*), suppleness (*Losgelassenheit*), contact (*Anlehnung*), impulsion (*Schwung*), straightening (*Geraderichten*), and collection (*Versammlung*) — are interdependent.

The elements of the scale of training are goals we want to reach. They apply to all dressage work including starting the young horse, correcting a mistrained horse, and training movements at all levels. Every daily training session is organized by these goals. The elements of the scale of training remain the same for other riding disciplines, though we might use different exercises or emphasize one goal over another.

Rhythm and suppleness are the foundation for all training. Out of suppleness we develop contact. When we have gained contact, we can work on impulsion. With impulsive riding, we can straighten the horse. The straightened horse gives us the possibility of achieving collection. The scale of training already plays a role during the green horse's first lungeing lessons, even before we start riding. We try to achieve those goals systematically to help the horse perform the desired dressage movements with a supple body and mind. The final goal is a submissive horse. The degree of the horse's submissiveness increases as he progresses to higher training levels.

THE (TRAINING) PHASES

*Training or accustoming phase/*Gewoehnungsphase

The first phase of the scale of training is the training or accustoming phase. In this phase the horse is trained to become accustomed to carrying the rider with a supple body — without tensing or cramping any muscles and without resistance. He must gain trust in the rider and his work. During this phase the rider first establishes a steady rhythm in all paces and movements. Legs that push rhythmically and hands that are elastic and positioned low are essential. We do not collect the horse at this stage because he does not have the strength and physical ability. Achieving rhythm is the basis for all continuing work.

The second important element at this time is suppleness. The basis for physical suppleness is mental relaxation and contentedness. Establish suppleness at the start of every riding session. A horse with a tensed back, disturbed rhythm, no or incorrect mouth activity, crookedness, or inadequate activity in the hind legs lacks suppleness.

The next element of the training phase is contact. During the warm-up of every session, we ride with very soft and carefully obtained contact, especially with the young horse. This best enables the horse to find rhythm, balance, and suppleness.

We mainly ride the horse in a natural, basic trot on big lines while in the training phase. We generally accept the speed the horse offers. The rider does not want to collect or extend the pace immoderately — unless the horse is extremely lazy and slow. Then we would ask for a different speed. If the horse hurries, we ride a slower pace. If the horse is lazy, we drive forward to obtain a better pace.

Many riders misunderstand how to drive the horse forward. They often merely quicken the speed. This results in a hurried footfall and disturbance of the rhythm. Driving a horse forward to achieve rhythm and a good gait does not mean increasing the speed but engaging the horse's hind legs to carry weight and step forward energetically.

We do not actively work on the walk. We mainly walk on a loose rein, shortening the reins only briefly in preparation for an exercise. As walk does not have impulsion, you can very easily ruin this gait. Start working the canter when the horse offers it easily.

Phase of development of the driving power of the hind legs/ **Entwicklung der Schubkraft**

In the continuing training of the horse, we improve contact and activate the horse's hind legs more to move them farther toward the horse's center of gravity. We develop the forward-driving power of the hind legs.

Added to the criteria of rhythm, suppleness, and contact, we work on impulsion and straightening. Acquiring the driving power of the hind legs is a prerequisite for the later development of the carrying power of the horse's hindquarters.

Now the contact on the reins and the position of head and neck slowly change. The continuous raising of the forehand increasingly develops the body posture the horse needs for higher levels. It is crucial to develop impulsion first. Then the horse will be able to round his neck more and become supple in the poll. The noseline comes closer to the vertical.

Phase of the development of the carrying power of the hind legs/
Entwicklung der Tragkraft

To develop carrying power of the hind legs, the horse must have gained driving power. The rhythm in all gaits must be secure; the horse must be supple and in contact. Achieving impulsion brings with it the degree of submissiveness necessary for straightening and collection.

A horse without a rider will naturally carry more of his own weight on the front legs. The front legs serve as supports, while the hind legs create the forward motion. This balance is satisfactory as long as the horse does not have to carry the weight of a rider, which the horse will naturally try to carry on the forehand.

To keep him sound, we need to rebalance the horse so that his hind legs carry the weight instead. Through the forward-driving aids, especially the leg aids, we encourage his hind legs to step farther forward toward the center of gravity to carry more weight. We achieve this by collecting the horse.

As a result, the joints of the hind legs flex more, are lifted higher, and are set farther forward, carrying more weight. The increased engagement of the hind legs means that the forehand carries less weight and elevates. This causes the horse's head and neck to be carried in a higher position. This is what we call collection.

With the increasing bend of the haunches, the rider can "shorten" the horse. Half halts in combination with the forward-driving aids bring the horse's hind legs more under the center of gravity and make them carry more weight. Therefore, a certain amount of collection is healthy for every horse.

Engaging the hind legs is a gradual process. We do not work on or talk about collection during the beginning training stages. Every horse needs to gain physical strength to achieve collection.

THE SIX ELEMENTS

*Rhythm/*Takt is the absolute equality of motion in time and measurement in all gaits. All steps must be of equal length and timing. Every gait must have a clear hoof beat — four beats in walk, two beats in trot, three beats in canter. The horse must remain in rhythm whether he is on straight or bent lines.

The young horse has natural balance, which we disturb when we mount the horse for the first time. The horse needs to rebalance during training. He must learn to adjust his center of gravity with the rider on his back in all situations. The rider must have control over seat and aids to be able to support the horse in finding his balance.

Moving in rhythm helps the young horse recover his balance. Without rhythm, training cannot proceed correctly. You must know the sequence of footfalls of every gait to be able to judge and improve rhythm. When irregularities in the rhythm occur, you need to return to work that is more basic to solve the problem. Rhythm is absolutely necessary for continuing work.

To improve rhythm, we do more bending work, ride transitions, and practice the movement "letting the horse stretch forward-downward on the reins"/*Zuegel aus der Hand kauen lassen.* Correct lungeing, as well as trail riding, cavaletti work, or jumping small obstacles with plenty of dressage work in between, will help him to gain rhythm.

The four beats of the walk must occur at equal distance and timing as the four feet step forward. Disturbances of the walk may occur as irregular steps or a loss of the four-beat sequence, leading to a "pace-like" walk or even a pace. Horses with a naturally excellent walk with long steps are especially prone to pacing.

In trot each diagonal pair of legs moves simultaneously. A common irregularity of rhythm is when the hind legs reach the ground later than the respective front legs. Usually these horses have been introduced to collection prematurely, with insufficiently gymnasticized hindquarters.

The most severe disturbance of rhythm in trot shows in frequently occurring short, uneven steps. The horse steps far less forward with one hind leg than the other. On first sight, it seems as if the horse is lame on one front leg. We call this "rein-lameness." These horses trot rhythmically without a rider. The cause is a rider who uses one rein much more strongly than the other and generally rides with too strong rein aids and insufficient driving aids. The horse does not supple on the bit on one side, and the rider keeps too much pressure on this rein. The rider must change the influence on this rein, giving more often and, overall, leading more sensitively on this side.

In canter we must have a clear three beats and equal time between strides. The respective diagonal pair of legs, inside hind and outside front, must move simultaneously. If the inside hind touches the ground before the diagonal front, we have the faulty "four-beat" canter. This mistake occurs primarily because of excessive restraining rein aids without sufficient forward-driving aids.

We need to feel that the horse lets the rider push — he waits for the forward-driving leg aids. We do not want any hastened or hesitant steps.

Suppleness/**Losgelassenheit** is the physical and mental relaxation of the horse. The horse moves in rhythm, calmly, without hurrying, and with sufficient length of stride. The horse willingly stretches head and neck forward-downward and carries the tail without tension. The swinging back allows the rider to sit comfortably. The horse waits for and anticipates the rider's driving aids.

Suppleness is the foundation for all training. You have gained suppleness when the horse readily stretches head and neck forward-downward in all gaits whenever asked to, with energetically moving hind legs and a swinging back. Now all muscles of the physically and mentally supple horse contract and stretch alternately, with the necessity of motion. There is no tightness but instead an elastic tension.

Suppleness means physical comfort and mental balance. There are many obvious signs indicating that a horse moves with suppleness and relaxation. You observe suppleness in the contented, yet concentrated, expression of the horse's eyes and ears, the regularly swinging back, and the even bending and stretching of the joints. The tail is carried relaxed and swings softly. The horse keeps his mouth shut, gently chewing on the bit.

The physically and mentally relaxed horse will snort softly from time to time, which is a sign of unrestricted breathing, possible only when the back muscles are relaxed. The snorting sound will occur when the horse exhales, showing that he is breathing deeply and slowly.

In comparison, the tense horse stiffens his neck and back muscles and is uncomfortable and bouncy to sit. Usually the horse is not correctly on the bit and is using the wrong neck muscles, which keeps his neck very stiff. The tail stays pressed down or tilted to one side and doesn't swing. If the horse is also mentally tense, his ears will show his agitation, and he may swish his tail. The tense horse's pace is unrhythmic, with either hurried or dragging and uneven steps. He may jig or pace when extremely tense.

To improve suppleness, we do posting trot and transitions from trot to canter and back. We can do cavaletti work, riding uphill on trails, and lungeing. The slightly more advanced horse is ridden in leg-yields in walk, and turns on the forehand. The evidence for suppleness is the horse's swinging back and his search for a soft contact on the bit. In the movement *Zuegel aus der Hand kauen lassen*, the horse must stretch forward-down-ward without quickening or pulling the reins. The leg-yielding is in rhythm and not hurried.

Loss of suppleness can occur when the rider starts with new move-ments. Here, it is important to stay calm and regain inner and outer sup-pleness. Take walk breaks and make changes to well-known basic work. Sometimes you will find horses that hardly supple at all. This can have phys-ical reasons, like pain, sore muscles, or conformation problems. Mental rea-sons may be fear, nervousness, temperament, or bad experiences.

Contact/**Anlehnung** occurs when the horse moves willingly and equally between both reins and legs. Contact is the soft but steady connection between the rider's hand and the horse's mouth. In a willing, rhythmic, and supple forward movement, the horse searches for contact.

The German word for this is *anlehnung*, which means to lean on, a good description for the kind of contact we desire. In the supple, forward-moving horse, the impulsion of the hind legs will travel over the swinging back and relaxed poll into the steady and softly restraining hands of the rider. The forward-driving aids, back, and legs create contact by pushing the horse into the reins.

To understand why we want the horse on the bit, imagine carrying a sack on your shoulders like a backpack. Carrying the sack with a hollow back makes it feel heavier and hard to balance. Sooner or later your back will hurt. Now round your back, stretching head and neck forward-downward. The burden feels lighter. You are in balance, and carrying the weight becomes comfortable.

When the young horse stretches forward-downward in his head and neck, he lifts the muscles that go along his back. These muscles carry and balance the rider. Now his back muscles are free to act their intended way — contracting and stretching rhythmically.

A horse that uses the muscles this way will allow you to sit comfortably because his back is swinging. A horse with a high head and neck carriage and a hollow, tense back has a shortened stride, which will feel uncomfortably bouncy to you. It is not an accident that a horse looks nice when on the bit. The horse's head-neck lever balances the rider's weight, leaving the muscles of the back and croup for their job — forward movement.

Despite neck muscles being made for longer contraction, they still need to be prepared for this job. When a young horse starts jerking his head and neck upward after approximately twenty to thirty minutes of being on the bit, the reason is not disobedience but fatigue or soreness. Do not correct roughly or use draw reins or some other aid. Let your horse rest and stretch his neck for a few minutes or quit riding for the day.

As the horse progresses through the dressage training stages, his head and neck position will change from long and low to the more advanced elevated position, but he will remain on the bit.

Do not take contact with restraining rein aids only. This would only be a forced shaping of the horse's head and neck position. A correct contact gives the rider equal pressure on both reins, with the horse leaning onto the reins, not leaning on them with much weight. When the horse takes considerable support on the reins, the rider must work with a lot of giving rein aids to prevent the horse from propping on the reins.

During training phase we work on achieving contact without riding the horse "on the bit" by force. Every forceful influence disturbs the supple activity of mouth, back, and hindquarters. Soft contact is crucial for gaining sensitive hands. Only use the restraining rein enough to use the power of the driving aids to bring the horse to a contact. During the different training stages, the horse is in contact in different head and neck positions. For basic training, we ride the young horse in a very low position. The horse's mouth is about level with the horse's point of shoulder. His neck is still in a longer frame, so we achieve the necessary stretching and relaxation of the neck and back muscles. The poll must always be the highest point, except when we let the horse stretch forward-downward on the reins. As training advances, head and neck assume increasingly higher positions.

Transitions and lengthening and shortening the stride in trot and canter are movements that bring the horse into contact. The rider does this with soft hands holding the driving power slightly back. With good contact, the horse keeps his mouth closed and softly chews (not bites) on the bit. We observe foaming saliva around the horse's lips, signifying the horse is supple in the poll. In an effort to achieve contact, faulty head and neck positions often appear. The horse may get behind, above, or against the bit, behind the vertical, or a "broken neck" may develop. (See chapter 11 for definitions.)

Impulsion/Schwung is the driving power of the hind legs in the forward motion. A horse with impulsion moves forward energetically with his

hind legs swinging far forward. Impulsion prolongs the moment of suspension. The back swings elastically.

Immediately after the hind leg leaves the ground, the hock bends energetically forward and upward. A horse is using his hock joint incorrectly
when he only lifts it upward or lifts it upward and backward. The hind legs
are "left behind," a sign of lack of impulsion. The haunches, consisting of
hip and stifle joints, bend and stretch more. The swinging back muscles of
the horse let the rider sit comfortably and ride the forward motion. The
supple and submissive horse gets more expressive gaits and softer contact
through increasing impulsion.

Only trot and canter — gaits with a moment of suspension — can have
impulsion. Some horses are naturally talented with very impulsive gaits.
You will only need to improve them. Other horses must become more flexible and supple in their haunches first to develop more impulsion. Gaits
with expressive impulsion signify the well-ridden horse.

A common mistake is to hurry the horse in a quickened pace to achieve
impulsion. This will lead to shorter, quicker steps and a shortened moment
of suspension. The horse may still move in rhythm, but we will lose impulsion. The horse also may react with tense "artificial steps" so that the
moment of suspension takes longer, but the horse's legs do not cover more
ground. The correct reaction to our work should be a prolonged moment
of suspension with the horse's hind legs swinging farther forward and covering more ground. The rider must gain the feeling that the horse "takes
him into the forward motion."

To improve impulsion, we ride transitions and changes in pace with
extensions to medium trot and medium canter. The rider must take care
to do all transitions in rhythm, especially down transitions. Give sensitive
rein aids, so you do not disturb the horse's hind legs swinging forward.

Straightening/Geraderichten is working against the natural crookedness of the horse by bringing the horse's forehand in front of his hind legs.
This aligns the longitudinal axis of the horse on the track you are riding,
no matter if it is a straight or bent line.

Straightening means the horse is straight in his longitudinal axis on a straight line and bent in his axis on a bent line, so that each hind leg moves into the track of the lateral front leg. You will be able to have even contact on both reins. There is no tilt in the horse's head; both ears are even. The rider can perform circles and voltes equally on both sides and is able to keep an evenly balanced seat on the horse.

Straightening is the necessary preparation for collection. It makes the hind legs equally capable of carrying weight. Only in a straightened horse will the hind legs work over back, neck, and poll into the rider's hands. This means the impulsion we create by driving the hind legs is controlled by the hands, which in turn influence the hind again. A straightened horse is obedient and submissive.

In the straightened horse each hind leg moves into the track of the lateral front leg. Every horse is born with a crooked body posture, comparable to our left- or right-handedness. We call it "natural crookedness," which means the unevenness of the body's left and right sides in muscle strength and elasticity. When we gymnasticize the horse to use both sides of his body evenly, he will perform movements without wearing one side out.

The horse's forehand is naturally narrower than his hindquarter. If we observe a square-standing horse from the front, we will see four feet. But when observing a correctly trained and straightened dressage horse we will only see two feet. Straightening work will narrow the hind legs' track.

In young or untrained horses, the hind legs do not move exactly in the direction of the same front leg. In most cases, the left hind leg steps toward the space between the front legs. The right hind leg moves toward the outside of the right front leg, so it is beside and not under the horse's body. As a result, the horse puts more weight on his left shoulder, tensing the left neck muscle so the rider has stronger contact on the left rein. The horse tries to avoid contact on the right rein, hollowing the neck on this side. This unevenness forces the left hind leg to bend the joints more and the right hind to develop more impulsion. The left front foot is burdened more, so the danger of premature wear exists. If work is continued without straightening, only the left hind leg will function well and the right hind leg will try to move to the side even more.

When the horse is crooked to the right like this, the rider must drive stronger with the right leg to prevent the right hind leg from moving toward this side. The left leg drives to encourage the left hind to extend forward more. The left rein guards the left shoulder, the right rein leads the forehand toward the right until the right front leg is in front of the right hind.

To straighten the horse, work on bent lines and lateral movements that correspond with the horse's training stage. We always want to bring the horse's forehand in front of the hindquarter. Of the lateral movements, we mainly ride the shoulder-in to straighten. This erases tenseness in the poll and makes the neck muscles of both sides evenly supple and movable. It flexes the horse's back and vertebrae to bring the hind legs to step forward underneath the weight. Hip, stifle, and hock joints are flexed more. All body muscles get supple and equally strong. We ride younger horses on circles, older ones on voltes, turns on the haunches, and serpentines and figure eights in trot. With the advanced horse we do this bending work also in canter and add counter canter.

The horse often will tilt his head in the poll. Carrying the inside hand (on the side of the lower standing ear) higher helps temporarily. The rider's inside leg must push slightly stronger to engage the inside hind leg and achieve the bend in the longitudinal axis. The rider must release rein pressure often on the side the horse leans on strongly. Try to take up more rein contact on the other side. Given enough impulsion, the horse will follow the rider's command to move on bent lines better.

As a result, the horse searches for both reins evenly, front and hind legs move in the same track on straight and bent lines, and submissiveness increases. At advanced training stages we use lateral movements to straighten the horse. Ineffective straightening work shows in the tilting of the poll, an exaggerated flexion of head and neck and insufficient bend in the longitudinal axis.

Collection/Versammlung means bending the horse's haunches more to make the hind legs more active and able to carry more weight. Collection increases submissiveness.

When you activate the horse's hind legs to step under the center of gravity, you'll get the feeling of riding uphill. The forehand of the horse rises, which raises the poll and neck and frees the front legs. We say the "forehand raises" or the "horse moves in an elevated position." (See chapter 11 for their definitions.) The dressage rider uses movements and transitions to engage the horse to carry more of his and the rider's weight with his hind legs.

You can influence the horse's hindquarters with your rein aids in combination with dominating forward-driving back and leg aids, which will engage the hind legs to step forward more and carry more weight. Carrying more weight, the haunches get gymnasticized. The joints bend more strongly, so the hindquarters lower and the forehand raises. The increased bending and stretching of the hindquarter joints result in more elevated and cadenced steps. The steps cover less ground with no loss of impulsion and prolonged suspension. The horse automatically carries head and neck in a higher position when the hindquarters lower, and you will feel a softer contact on the reins. The horse will move in "self-carriage" (see chapter 11).

As we can only strengthen the forehand to a certain extent, we must collect the ridden horse to keep him more healthy and balanced. Collection creates increased reactions and higher performance capabilities. This not only applies to the dressage horse but to others as well, although the kind of work will determine the appropriate amount of collection and the way to train. We collect the hunting horse in critical situations, the trail horse on difficult ground, or the jumper in front of high obstacles. You will reach collection only with correct, systematic, and patient training.

We start training collection with the more advanced horse when he approaches second level. Before this, he is physically unable to do collection without being forced. He may become sore or injured. During the initial training of collection, we only ride collected in trot or canter for short periods to prevent tiring or overworking the horse. Collection takes much more strength than all the work we did before. Ride collected walk sparingly and with great care. Regularly break up collected work with extensions to working or extended paces to create forwardness again. We ride many transitions to collect on straight and bent lines. The forward-driving aids create impulsion that we hold back by restraining rein aids without restricting the hind legs from swinging forward. The restraining rein transfers the increased driving power of the hind into carrying power — the horse is collected. A major mistake is using very strong rein aids but no or insufficient driving aids. Then the steps get shorter, but we lose impulsion. Eventually irregularities of the paces occur.

Medium trot in between collected work is a touchstone of training. Use it to verify the correctness of your work. If the medium trot develops with regular, expressive steps, the former work was correct. Transitioning back to collected trot, the horse transfers the gained impulsion of the extended pace into more cadenced steps. If the horse leans too strongly on the reins, resists the leg, or loses rhythm in extended gaits, the collected work was either too long or performed incorrectly.

Successful mastery of the three phases results in a correctly trained horse. Whenever you need to find out if a horse has correct dressage training, do not look for any movements, but check for the following conditions: Is the horse in even contact on both reins? Does he move rhythmically and freely forward? Are his poll and back supple and his mouth correctly active, softly chewing on the bit and developing foam around the lips? Does he move correctly on straight and bent lines? Does he react submissively to half halts? Can you extend or collect the pace at all times? Does the horse stretch forward-downward on the reins whenever asked? When the horse reacts incorrectly in one of these points, the training foundation is not correct.

If the horse is able to do all this, he has a solid and correct training foundation. Even if there are movements still missing from his training, you will be able to train him easily and quickly.

9 | In the Arena

THE DRESSAGE ARENA

There are two different sizes of dressage arenas by which dressage tests and school figures are defined. These dimensions are acknowledged by the Fédération Equestre International, the international horse sports federation, and used by most member countries for their national show tests.

This does not mean that you should not ride in any other size arena. A bigger arena can offer more possibilities for varying the work and riding without constant contact with walls. Unless your arena is not extremely large, the ends should be half the length of the sides.

The standard large arena is 20 by 60 meters; the standard small arena is 20 by 40 meters. The perimeter of the arena is marked with letters or dots called markers or points. They are the same in both standard-sized arenas, although the 60-meter arena has more.

Letters marking spots on the centerline only appear on diagrams.

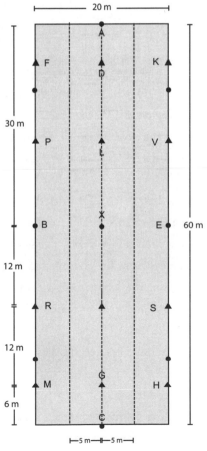

20-by-60-meter arena

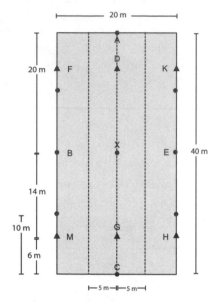

20-by-40-meter arena

Of the seven circle points, four are usually marked as white or black dots on the walls of the long sides, each one 10 meters away from the corners. Two are in the middle of the short sides at the letters A and C. The seventh circle point is understood to be in the center of the arena, where we also have the letter X. In the following diagrams you can see, for example, that they assist riding accurate 20-meter circles or serpentines with three loops.

The four letters M–F–H–K on the long sides of the arena, each 6 meters from the corners, are called changing points. We use them, for example, to ride a change of rein on the long or the short diagonal. From the corners they are 6 meters, which is approximately two horse lengths — exactly the distance a rider needs to prepare for a movement after having come through the corner.

The letters E and B mark the middles of the long sides, and the letters A and C mark the middle of the short sides.

The letters P–V–R–S are only on the long sides of the 60-meter arena, 18 meters from the corners and 12 meters from the middle (E and B) of each side. The letters D–L–I–G mark points on the centerline. These are additional markers to define where certain figures and movements are executed.

The dotted lines on the diagram show the quarter lines. There are three in an arena, each 5 meters apart. No markers identify these lines. The dotted line in the middle of each arena is the centerline, from A to C.

Riding on the first track means you ride right beside the arena wall. When you wish to work your horse away from the walls to learn the outside aids better, you move onto the **second track**. This must be far enough from the wall that the first track is left free (another horse is able to pass you on your outside).

To change rein or lead means riding a figure that makes you change direction. In an arena you ride either on the **left or right lead**, which signifies the direction you are riding. Riding through a corner in a left turn (your left hand shows to the center of the arena) is called being on the left lead.

When a command for a figure mentions letters at which the figure begins or finishes, you leave the track you are on when the horse's forehand is at this letter. You do the same thing when you end the figure, arriving at or returning to the track at the letter with the horse's forehand.

THE SCHOOL FIGURES

Knowing and practicing these school figures provides your training sessions with some variety and helps you understand your trainer's instructions. Asked in tests at dressage shows, school figures are helpful in showing the stage of training your horse has achieved. You can also better predict which way other riders in an arena may go by knowing these common figures. In training you can vary these figures or create new ones. Some of them are perfect to use in the warm-up phase. Those containing smaller turns with the necessary stronger bend and collection should only be ridden in the working phase after warm-up to have a positive effect and to avoid demanding too much at an early stage.

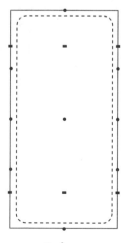

1. **To go large:** to ride around the whole arena. This is done on the left or right lead. Riding large means having a straight horse on the long and short sides and a horse bent to the inside in each corner, as on every bent line.

2. **Ride B–X–E (or E–X–B) with or with-**

Go large

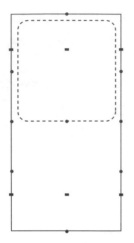

B-X-E (E-X-B) with/without
change of rein

out change of rein: Change of rein means to change the lead/direction you are riding. To ride exactly across the line from B over X to E, don't forget that the horse is almost 3 meters long (the official measurement for a horse length), so you need to begin the turn from the wall about one horse length before E or B in order to ride the turn and then be straight on the line across the arena. You need to prepare the turn at least two horse lengths before E or B, because the horse needs a moment to follow your command and then turn his body.

3. **Change on the centerline with/without change of rein:** To ride down the centerline, which is the line you can draw from A to C or vice versa. You begin the figure about one horse length before A or C. You need that distance to ride a turn the size of a quarter volte in order to meet the centerline. Upon arrival you can

Change on the centerline
with/without change
of rein

either turn into the direction you had before the figure or change the lead.

4. **Diagonal change of rein:** To perform a change of lead while riding across one of the long diagonals in the arena. The points to leave and to arrive are the changing points (M–F–K–H). This means to prepare while still in the corner so that the forehand of the horse is leaving or arriving exactly at those points. As the diagonal is a straight line, the horse must be

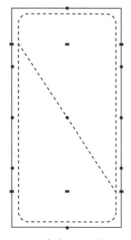

Diagonal change of rein

straight on the diagonal. Performing this movement you always ride a change of lead. Change of posting occurs one horse length before you arrive at the letter.

5. **Change of rein on a short diagonal:** To leave from the same point, M–F–H–K, as the diagonal change of rein, but arrive at either E or B. Again you leave and arrive with the horse's forehand at the points. You do a change of lead.

6. **Riding a 20-meter circle:** When you receive this instruction, initiate the circle at the next

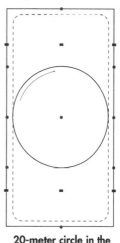

Change of rein on a short diagonal

opportunity. You start at the middle of the short side, A or C, and you do a circle from circle point to circle point. You can ride a 20-meter circle at A or C.

7. **Riding a 20-meter circle in the center of the arena:** We ride this circle in the middle of the arena with the letter X as the center. You start the center

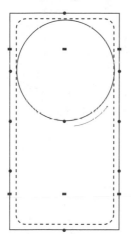

20-meter circle

circle at B or E.

8. **Change of rein through the circle:** Riding a change of lead inside the circle you are on while riding the figure of the letter S. You leave on one of the circle points from which the open side of the circle starts (the open side of circle is the one with no wall to the outside), and ride a half circle with 10-meter diameter. You change bend in the circle center, riding straight for about one horse length to change

20-meter circle in the middle

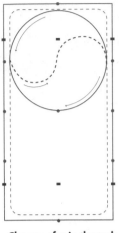

Change of rein through circle

flexion and bend in the horse and ride another half circle to arrive at the opposite circle point where the enclosed half of the circle starts.

9. **Change of rein from circle to circle:** You ride on one of the circles at A or C and turn at X onto the other, changing the horse's flexion and bend and, if necessary, your posting. When receiving commands from an instructor, you keep riding on the new circle after the change until a new figure is commanded.

10. **Volte/Circle with 6-, 8-, or 10-meter diameter:** A volte is a circle of 10 meters or less. To ride a volte correctly, you must arrive at exactly the same point that you left. Small voltes, figure eights or sharp turns (with a diameter of 6 meters or less) must only be ridden when the horse is warmed up and sufficiently submissive. Only then does the exercise have a positive effect.

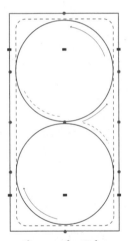

Change of rein from circle to circle

11. **Half circle with change of rein:** A half circle can be ridden at different points in the arena.

12. **Riding the figure eight:** Riding two circles/voltes of any size with a change of lead in the middle.

13. **One loop on the long side, 40-meter arena:** Leave at a changing point. Passing the circle point, the bend and direction of the line changes, so you change flexion and bend of your horse and your posting here. Coming to the end

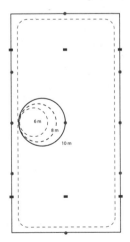

Volte of 6/8/10 meters

of the figure you do the same again, passing by the circle point. You arrive at the changing point. Passing by B or E, where you have the greatest distance to the wall, this distance should be 5 meters. In the 60-meter arena, we still leave and arrive at the changing points, but ride as far as X toward the center of the arena at the widest point.

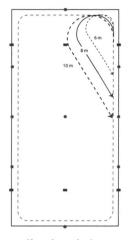

Half circle with change of rein

14. Two loops on the long side, 40-meter arena: These are ridden in the same procedure as the one loop. The widest part of each loop is 2.5 meters from the wall. Because of the quickness of the changes of bend, this is a figure for collected work and therefore more appropriate for horses at higher levels of training. Each time the direction changes, we must change the horse's flexion and bend. Two loops in a 60-meter arena are ridden five meters to the inside of the arena.

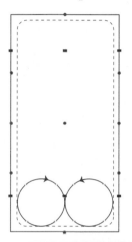

The figure eight

15. **Serpentine with three loops, each loop to touch the long side of the arena:** These serpentines consist of three equal half circles along the arena with short straight lines in between. The first loop starts on the short side of the arena, close before the corner, so it is cut flat. Leave the wall at a circle point with the horse's forehand (first half circle), ride straight over toward the opposite long side, do a half circle (second) at B or E and move back to

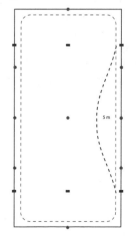

One loop on long side

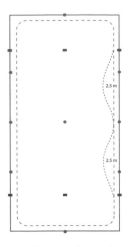

Two loops on long side

arrive at a circle point again (third half circle). With three loops you cross the centerline twice. Each time you have done a half circle, the horse is straightened for crossing the centerline and flexed and bent again into the new direction when you arrive at the beginning of the next half circle. The change of posting or the canter lead happens when crossing the centerline.

16. **Serpentine with four loops, each loop to touch the long side of the arena:** This serpentine is performed like the previous. The serpentine with four loops is more difficult to ride precisely because you always touch the wall between points. You leave the wall between changing and circle point (e.g., behind M), touch the opposite side between circle point and the middle of the long side (e.g., before E, but a little closer to E than to the circle point), then,

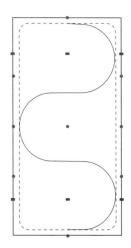

Serpentine with three loops

again, you touch the wall between the middle of long side and circle point (behind, but closer to B). Then you do the last loop and arrive finally at the wall between circle and changing point (before K), and the last loop is finished at A. Riding four loops always means a change of rein. You again change bend and posting riding across the centerline.

17. **Serpentine with five loops, each loop to touch the long side of the arena:** Here you leave the wall at the changing point (e.g., M),

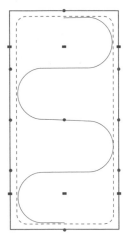

Serpentine with four loops

touch the wall at the circle point, touch at the middle of long side (B), touch circle point, and arrive finally at changing point (F). Changing of bend again when riding across centerline, you arrive on the same lead. Because five loops in a 40-meter arena are very sharp turns, you ride this figure only in sitting trot after the warm-up.

ARENA RULES

Knowing these rules and establishing them at the arena will make it easier to handle situations in which riders meet while training at

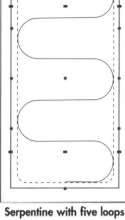

Serpentine with five loops

the same time. They will make your own training easier and prevent disturbances.

1. Before you enter an enclosed arena where several other riders are already working, you should wait in front of the entrance where you can see everything and announce clearly that you want to enter the arena (We ask, "Door/Entry free?"). One of the riders in the arena, usually the one closest to the entry, should then answer to let you know that he is paying attention (example: "Door/Entry is free!").

2. When you stop for any reason, you should stay in the middle of one of the circles, where you will least disturb anybody.

3. The faster gaits (trot and canter) have priority over the walk. When you walk your horse on the first track and other riders come toward you from the front or behind in a higher gait, you move to the inside of the arena to give way to them.

4. To go large has priority over riding on a circle.

5. The left lead has the right of way. If you are working on the left lead in trot or canter, those riders on the right lead and coming toward you must move to the inside to leave the first track to you. However, the rider walking always has to give way to the faster gaits, independent from the lead he is on.

6. You should always keep a safe distance of about one horse length from others. When passing another rider or following another horse maintain this safe distance. Maintain this distance especially when you do not know the other horse or what his rider intends to do. It helps prevent bouncing into somebody or getting hurt by a kicking or bucking horse.

10 | **Movements**

Movements are clearly defined exercises that we use to improve the horse's physical and mental fitness and to make him submissive and obedient to our aids. Training advances as movements build on each other in difficulty, though their order may vary with the individual horse.

Divide the learning process of each movement into several stages, and have a goal at each stage — don't expect the horse to perform the whole movement perfectly right away. For example, when you begin to teach the leg-yield to the horse, your first goal should be only that he yield from your leg for a few steps. Don't worry if he is above the bit and not flexed yet. When he understands what your sideways-pushing leg commands, your next goal can be the right head position. If you ask for everything at once, the horse will resist and become tense.

It depends on the individual horse whether a movement will be easy or difficult, at which stage we can introduce it, and how often we may repeat it during a session. Pace, impulsion, and probable collection depend on the movement we work. Some of the movements are basic and help warm up the horse, others are ridden only during working phase of a session and at the appropriate training level.

RIDING BENT LINES

You know you ride bent lines when you do loops and serpentines, but you are on a bent line as well when you just ride through a corner of the arena. Doing this correctly means you have to know what to do and what to look for.

As much as anatomy allows it, the horse is bent in his longitudinal axis according to the bent line he is on. The lateral front and hind legs move on

Bending on the circle

the same track, meaning the hind leg follows exactly the lateral front. The inside hind leg carries more weight. The horse is straightened according to the bent line. Imagine a horse that stays more or less straight in his body. He will take the bent line like a bus. While the front end is turning, the hind end swings to the outside. If the horse does this, he will get off the rider's aids and move unbalanced.

Like the horse, we have to move our body into the direction of the turn to stay aligned with the horse. Our shoulders and pelvis must rotate. To achieve a better feel and understanding for this rotating motion, walk (on your own feet) and then turn to the side. Feel how you automatically turn your body into the direction of the motion. Your inside hip moves forward, as well as your outside shoulder; your inside shoulder comes back.

This very same motion, which we usually perform unconsciously whenever we turn while moving, must occur when we ride a turn with the horse. This way our shoulders and hips stay parallel to the horse's. Rotating our body into the direction of the turn also automatically shifts our weight more strongly to the inside seat bone. Riders often forget to turn their upper body toward the outside. To experience what the horse feels when we do this, take a few steps and turn while purposely shifting your upper body toward the outside and also looking there. Feel how awkward and difficult the turn gets. Now the reins tell the horse to turn one way and the rider's upper body and weight aid telegraph the opposite direction. This confusion generally creates resistance in the turn. Finely tuned horses will do turns with the aid of body rotation and the connected weight only.

RIDING VOLTES

Voltes are small circles of 10 meters or less. Up to first/second level of training, we only ride voltes of 10 meters to enable the horse to do them correctly.

In higher levels, we ride voltes of 6 meters or 8 meters in collected paces. Moving in a volte, the horse needs the largest possible amount of bend in his longitudinal axis. As on other bent lines, the horse is supposed to be "straightened on the bent line." The hind legs follow the track of the lateral front legs. Riding a volte less than 6 meters, it is almost impossible for the horse to fit his bend according to the bend of the volte, as his anatomy limits him. The hindquarters drift outward and disturb the rhythm.

INSTRUCTIONS:

Ride voltes with the same aids as circles. The volte has to end at exactly the same point it started. The rider has to be even more careful to ride them evenly rounded. Ellipse-shaped voltes are a common mistake.

The half circle with change of rein, which is also a volte for most of the figure, is started out like a volte. From the widest part of it (after about half of the circle/volte), we proceed in a sloping line back to the track.

MISTAKES:

The inside rein is often used too strongly to lead the horse around the volte with not enough guarding-rein aid on the outside rein. This can cause outward-swinging quarters, disturbances of rhythm, the horse's head coming behind the vertical, and resistance against the reins because of imbalance.

RIDING THROUGH A CORNER

Each corner is like a quarter of a volte and ridden like one.

INSTRUCTIONS:

1. Flex and bend the horse to the inside just before reaching the corner.

2. The inside rein gives the flexion and the inside leg gives the bend in the longitudinal axis, while the outside rein and leg act as guarding aids.

3. The rider's weight is stronger on the inside seat bone to engage the horse's inside hind leg to move underneath his center of gravity and carry

weight sufficiently. The horse is framed between the diagonal aids.

MISTAKES:

If the horse tries to flatten the corner more than you want, use your inside weight and leg aids more strongly to push the horse farther into the corner while half halting him with the outside rein. Do not forget that your horse is one horse length long, so if you bring his forehand too much into the corner, he will lose his balance by moving onto the outside shoulder.

TRAINING TIPS:

How deeply we ride into the corner depends on the horse's training level. The less trained the horse, the more flatly we ride the corner. Up to first level we ride voltes no smaller than 10 meters, meaning we flatten the corners so we ride a quarter volte of 10 meters.

In second level we ride deeper into the corner, making a quarter volte of about 8 meters and increase this in the higher levels to 6 meters. We flatten the corner more when riding a young horse to avoid using the aids too much and to keep within his physical and mental abilities. In lower training stages we flatten the corner slightly during the warm-up phase and demand more during the later work in accordance with the suppleness of the horse.

RIDING CHANGES OF REIN/LEAD ON THE FULL OR SHORT DIAGONAL OR THE CENTERLINE

Changing lead on the full or short diagonal, we have a bent line before reaching a straight.

INSTRUCTIONS:

1. As you ride through the corner, you already have the inside flexion and bend necessary to ride the turn.

2. Apply the inside leg and outside rein so the horse does not leave the track before his outside shoulder is at the changing point.

3. After the turn, straighten the horse, as you are on a straight line until you arrive at the diagonal changing point.

4. Here, again enter the first track when the horse's outside shoulder is at the arrival point.

MISTAKES:

Horses tend to drift to the inside when arriving at the changing point. If that happens, focus on arriving at an imaginary point a few feet before the arrival point and apply much guarding leg on the drift side.

TRAINING TIPS:

Turning onto and leaving the centerline, we have to ride a turn equal to a quarter volte while we keep the horse straight on the centerline. We do not ride this figure too early in a training session.

RIDING ON A CIRCLE

As a circle is an evenly rounded line, you must ride it consistently. The horse stays continuously flexed and bent to the inside, framed by the rider's diagonal aids.

INSTRUCTIONS:

1. The inside rein gives flexion and the inside leg stays at the girth, keeping the bend and preventing the horse from turning in.

2. Keep the outside rein and the outside leg farther back as guarding aids to fence the horse's outside shoulder and hind leg.

MISTAKES:

Horse and rider often drift outward, unconsciously making "corners" on the circle line. Correct this by riding from one circle point to another, preparing to turn to the next before you reach the one in front of you.

TRAINING TIPS:

Working the horse on the circle with periods of counter flexion helps horse and rider to ride correct circles. Here, the rider's outside aids shift toward the inside of the circle. This exercise helps horses that tend to drift outward with their hindquarters or entire bodies. The rider achieves a better feeling for the great importance of his outside guarding rein and leg as their influence gets more obvious.

TURNS, LOOPS, SERPENTINES

Riding single or double loops on the long side, serpentines, and turns while changing from one circle to another, we switch the direction of a bent line.

INSTRUCTIONS:

1. Every time you switch direction, straighten the horse briefly for about one horse length before you flex and bend into the new direction. You ride straight for a longer distance in serpentines.

2. When you do changes of bend in posting trot, you also have to change the diagonal you post on.

3. Straighten the horse by shortening the new inside rein and releasing the new outside rein slightly.

4. Flex and bend in the new direction. Shift weight onto the new inside seat bone.

5. Bring the new inside leg forward into the forward-driving position. Move the new outside leg back into guarding position and change diagonal if posting.

In short: change seat, rein, flexion, and bend. Depending on the number of loops and their width, these are warm-up movements or preparation for collection.

DECREASING AND INCREASING THE CIRCLE

In this movement we change the size of the circle we ride on by decreasing and increasing it.

INSTRUCTIONS:

1. Start on a 20-meter circle. Slowly decrease the size of the circle by riding it smaller each round by about a track until you reach a circle the size of a volte (6–10 meters).

2. Remain there for a moment before you increase the circles round by round until you are back on the line of a 20-meter circle.

3. Apply the inside rein to flex and, therefore, lead the horse into the smaller circles. Use the outside guarding rein and leg aids for support.

TRAINING TIPS:

Ridden correctly — not by pulling and holding the horse in smaller circles with the inside rein — this movement helps improve the combined use of inside and outside aids and the horse's reactions to them.

TRANSITIONS

Transitions are changes from one gait to another or changes within a gait. The rider's actively used forward-driving aids engage the horse's hind legs either to collect or lengthen the stride. Work on your transitions often so they happen as promptly and accurately as any movement.

Transition into a higher gait

INSTRUCTIONS:

1. To prepare the horse and get his attention, use half halts before giving the necessary aids for the desired gait.

2. Start a walk from a halt by pushing with both legs at the same time. The leg aids to trot and canter are the same as during those gaits.

3. The moment the horse moves up into the higher gait, the rider releases rein pressure.

Transition into a lower gait

INSTRUCTIONS:

1. To transition into a lower gait, give some small half halts to prepare the horse and shorten the length of his stride before the transition.

2. You now give a sequence of stronger half halts, slowing the rhythm of your forward-swinging hips and applying soft pressure with the leg aid along with a restraining or taking-rein aid.

MISTAKES:

Many riders wrongly assume that a good down transition must be abrupt, which takes the fluency and harmony out of it. The opposite is letting the transition fade; the horse reacts so slowly and minimally that the transition is no longer clear. Find the medium between abrupt and fading, which would be a gradual but still prompt transition. Remember, the horse needs several strides for a down transition to decrease speed and shorten each stride.

If the horse starts throwing his head up when the reins restrain the forward motion, keep pushing, continue the gait, half halt, then try the down transition again. Do this as often as needed until the horse stays obedient on the rein aids then goes down in gait.

TRAINING TIPS:

Try to use a maintaining/restraining-rein aid instead of a taking rein to bring the horse into the lower gait. The maintaining rein holds back the horse's motion but allows the hind legs to step underneath the weight and shorten the stride with a supple back. A too strong taking-rein aid may cause the horse to step short in the hind legs and brake onto the front legs. With progressive training you will be able to move from a taking rein to a maintaining rein. Sitting "slower" or more passively in your back aid is the best way you can use your body to tell the horse to change gait.

During the initial training of down transitions, allow plenty of distance to come down into the lower gait. This gives the horse more time to under-stand and react without overusing your rein aid.

Transitions inside a gait

There are several possibilities for transitions inside a gait. We can lengthen and shorten the stride, collect and extend, and ride near halts (half halts).

INSTRUCTIONS:

1. To extend the gait or lengthen the strides, give half halts to prepare the horse, then use your leg and back aids more actively to engage the horse. Release the reins sufficiently to allow him to stretch his neck and thus lengthen the frame while still having contact with the horse's mouth.

2. To bring the horse back from a lengthened or extended stride, use half halts again and enough leg aid to prevent the horse from leaning on the reins and putting all his weight on the forehand.

3. To collect or shorten a gait, use taking- and giving-rein aids with for-ward-driving back and leg aids (the back aid is active but its rhythm is slightly slower than before). When you collect the horse, you shorten the strides but also make them more elevated and expressive.

4. To lengthen or shorten the strides, just ask for a slight difference in

the length of stride compared to the working pace.

Horse and rider are ready to work on extending and collecting the gaits when the horse stays rhythmic in the working paces and lengthens and shortens the strides fairly easily.

THE NEAR HALT

The near halt is a shortening/collecting of the pace for a few steps and then an immediate driving forward into the former pace. It is used in trot and canter.

INSTRUCTIONS:

Apply several half halts in a collecting manner inside one gait to collect or shorten stride for a couple of moments followed by a giving hand and forward-driving aids to bring the horse back to the former pace.

We use the near halt to gain more submissiveness, increase engagement and impulsion of the hindquarters, and teach the horse the first strides in collection.

This exercise is the "half halt" in German dressage terminology.

THE HALT/FULL HALT

The transition to a halt is called full halt. A full halt is the more intense applying of several half halts to bring the horse to a halt. You can start a full halt from every gait and every pace.

At the halt, the horse is standing absolutely motionless and straight on all four feet. The horse stands squarely with his hind legs under his center of gravity. The horse stays in self-carriage and on the rider's aids. The rider keeps the horse in a soft enclosure of his aids.

You can ride halts from the walk during the warm-up phase. You can also use the halt with young horses during early training. To make a good transition to the halt from other gaits, the horse needs a certain amount of training and suppleness.

INSTRUCTIONS:

1. Use several half halts to prepare and then execute the full halt. Give

the preparing half halts with a softly taking- and giving-rein aid to gain the horse's attention and test his submissiveness.

2. Depending on the horse's training level and submissiveness, the horse is pushed with the last one or two half halts against a restraining rein, using stronger driving aids than before.

3. If the restraining rein is not sufficient, a strong taking-rein aid is applied.

4. In the last instant before the horse actually stops, the rider releases the rein pressure (giving rein aid) to allow the horse to come to a square halt and keep balance and self-carriage.

5. Train square halts by riding the transition correctly. When the full halt improves, the square standing of the horse will automatically come.

The transition to the halt from whatever gait and speed must be fluent and harmonious, not abrupt or fading (too gradual).

MISTAKES:

The horse should not stand wide behind. Ride the transition more gradually, taking more steps before you finally come to the halt and using your leg aid more strongly.

The horse should not rest one leg. Drive stronger with your leg on the side where the horse does not step underneath his center sufficiently. At lower training stages the horse often keeps the weaker hind leg farther back to avoid carrying a lot of weight on it.

A major mistake is holding rein pressure until after the horse has stopped. This leads to a harsh, abrupt, and unharmonious transition in which the horse loses balance and does not stand square (or cannot stand square), pulls into the reins, and may step backward.

Many riders try to train their horses to a square halt by riding the full halts very abruptly and then correcting the standing horse with rein, leg, spur, or crop until he is standing square (or excited beyond control). There are two reasons for a halt that is not square. First, the horse is still green and has yet to learn. Younger horses often keep one hind leg resting or set back, or have unevenly placed front feet, because they have not yet balanced or become submissive enough to fulfill the rider's commands. So it may not be a sign of disobedience. Second, the rider often uses the rein aid too strongly and too long without releasing the pressure in time, therefore causing the horse to lose balance during the transition.

TRAINING TIPS:

Do not think of a full halt as a motion that can happen in one moment or step. Depending on the horse's speed, he needs several steps to brake to halt. Experience this for yourself to be aware: Jog or run and then halt while intensely feeling what your body does. Your "hind legs" first need to step on the ground more strongly to shorten the strides until you are able to halt. The faster the pace, the longer you need to stop.

Count about three to five steps as the minimum during which you bring the horse to a halt. This way you will also never have an abrupt stop again. Training yourself, count the half halts you give each step the horse makes with

The full halt

one, two, three. This method also helps the rider to check that he keeps his aids for a half halt only for the duration of horse's single step to stay in perfect rhythm with the motion.

When learning the halt, the younger horse will often not stand square or still and may even get nervous when the rider tries to use his aids to correct him. Try not to use the aids actively during the halt, no matter how the horse stands. Immobility itself is the first goal. The horse's ability to stand squarely will improve as the quality of his transition to the halt improves and his hindquarters strengthen.

TURN ON THE FOREHAND

The turn on the forehand is intended to teach the horse the sideways-pushing aids and to check his obedience to those aids. The horse makes a 180-degree turn with his hind legs moving around in a half circle while the front legs step almost in place with the inside front foot as the pivot. The inside hind leg steps in front and over the outside hind. The outside front leg moves around the inside front.

INSTRUCTIONS:

1. While introducing the turn on the forehand, halt along the outside wall on the second track. This gives the horse a visual borderline but also enough space for his head and neck and discourages him from backing up.

2. In preparation, bring the horse to a halt. Put more weight on the inside seat bone.

3. Flex the horse toward the wall and the sideways-driving leg. Remember we always flex and bend the horse to the inside, so the wall side will be the "inside."

4. Shorten the new inside rein to flex the horse's head and neck to this side. The outside rein acts as a guarding rein to prevent overflexing.

5. Bring weight on the inside seat bone.

6. Keep the inside leg slightly back to push the horse's rear around his front legs and apply pressure at each step. The outside leg is back in the guarding position to control the horse's outside hind leg and to prevent hurrying. Apply new leg aids for each of the horse's steps.

7. Ending the turn, soften on the inside

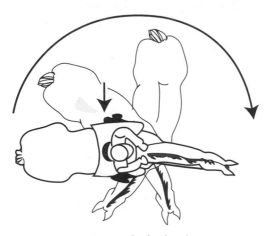

Turn on the forehand

aids and apply outside leg to halt the horse. Straighten the horse in head and neck

8. At later training stages you do the turn at various places in the arena.

MISTAKES:

When the horse is pulled around on the inside rein instead of pushed away from the inside leg, he usually turns more around his center instead. Use a stronger sideways-driving leg and less rein to correct this.

If the horse tries to move forward, restrain him with the reins; if the horse moves backward use both legs to drive him forward while slightly bracing the spine. Stepping forward is the greater mistake, as the horse resists the rider's aids here by moving against them.

You will lose your correct influence and shift your weight wrong if you lean toward the sideways-driving leg in the upper body. Do the turn on the forehand in front of a mirror so you can observe yourself.

The horse will rush around if the rider continuously squeezes with his inside leg. Use your leg in the rhythm of the motion, giving one push for each step of the horse. Also make sure your guarding outside leg is in place.

TRAINING TIPS:

While the horse is learning the movement, he can take a few steps backward during the turn as long as he yields the inside leg obediently. If he rushes, use less inside leg and more outside leg to slow down the motion.

When training the movement the very first time, do not use all aids at once. Combined aids might overwhelm and confuse the horse and cause resistance. Restrain on the inside rein rather than flex too much.

The turn on the forehand is the perfect movement to teach the inexperienced rider and horse about the coordination of several aids.

SUGGESTED EXERCISES:

Try the turn for about 90 degrees only, halt and pause, then either continue with the next 90 degrees or turn back the same way to the beginning position. This teaches the horse to be aware of and on the aids and teaches the rider to use his aids every moment.

A variation is to take one or two steps, halt, and stand still for a moment. Proceed with the next one or two steps until the full turn is completed.

As the movement is slow and easy to perform, a young horse can learn this very early, and it can be used as part of the warm-up. In addition, the beginner can practice coordinating his aids, especially those leading the horse sideways, and the feeling of controlling the horse's hind legs.

REIN BACK

In the rein back, the horse steps back with the diagonal pair of legs simultaneously (two-beat rhythm as in the trot, but without a moment of suspension), lifting his feet clearly off the ground. The backward steps should be of even length, ridden in a straight line, and performed willingly. In lower training levels, the horse has to step back about one horse length — about three to four steps. At the higher levels, a predetermined number of steps is required. If the horse is supposed to come to a halt after the rein back, the last step will be a half step in order to allow the horse to halt square.

Rein back is a check for submissiveness and obedience and improves these qualities. We must never misuse it to punish the horse. The joints of the hindquarters are bent more, so the rein back helps improve collection. Start it out slowly with young horses as they first have to get stronger and more coordinated. Teach the rein back only after the horse has gained an understanding and acceptance of the rider's aids. During the lower stages of training, we use rein back only after the warm-up phase. For the more advanced horse, you can rein back in the warm-up phase. If you start training and the horse becomes nervous and resistant, delay the movement until the horse has become more submissive.

INSTRUCTIONS:

1. In preparation to rein back, ride a halt with the horse standing square, straight, and on the aids.

2. Place your lower legs back in the guarding position to be prepared for a sideways swaying of the horse's rear.

3. With your weight equally on both seat bones, give the same leg pressure as when asking for a forward motion.

4. To change the impulse from forward to backward motion, take more rein pressure on both sides at exactly the moment the horse wants to move forward. The advanced horse will already react to a maintaining/restraining rein.

5. As soon as the horse reacts to your command, decrease the rein pressure while still keeping contact.

6. While the horse steps back, either stay passive or maintain your rein and leg aids, releasing them in between steps. Depending on the horse, use your legs in a left/right manner as in the walk or simultaneously.

7. To stop after the desired number of steps, use leg pressure on both sides with a slightly giving rein and brace your spine.

MISTAKES:

When a rider pulls back on the reins, usually the horse will react with a tensed back, stiffened hind legs, and strong resistance to any backward motion. When the horse rejects going backward, use only stronger leg aids or have someone help from the ground by using soft pushes or taps with a crop to the horse's chest or front fetlocks. Or, you can train the horse from the ground yourself. Keep the reins in one hand and the crop in the other while giving a voice command and soft taps with the crop on either the horse's chest or front feet. When the horse starts to understand the movement, try it again while riding. If the horse, especially a young one, has difficulties performing the movement, keep your weight more off the horse's back by temporarily sitting more on your thighs than your buttocks. Be careful not to lean forward or you will not regain your back aid in time to use it to stop the backward motion or prevent hurried steps.

A green horse often rushes backward with a tense back and as a result does not step back diagonally anymore, which counts as a major mistake in a test. Check that you do not use your rein aid too strong. Let the horse calmly rein back and accompany each step with your leg aids.

TRAINING TIPS:

If a horse refuses to step backward, start a turn on the forehand, using the rein a little more strongly. This will make the horse do one or two steps back, and you have a start. Here you use what would otherwise be a mistake — encouraging the horse to move backward in the turn.

The best preparation for a rein back under saddle is training the horse from the ground long before you ask while riding. Train the horse to back to a voice command and soft taps with a crop.

At advanced levels, we find the movement "alternated rein back/forward/rein back" (the German term *Schaukel*, which means "swing," defines the movement very well). Begin the movement from a halt. The horse steps back and walks forward several times, each move with a determined number of steps and no halt in between. Then continue in the predetermined gait without halting.

LEG-YIELDING

The horse moves forward and sideways showing four tracks with front and hind legs while the inside lateral pair is crossing over (moving forward and over) the outside pair. He is straight in his longitudinal axis and slightly flexed in head and neck toward your sideways-pushing leg, thus to the side opposite the direction of motion. The horse is at an angle of about 45 degrees to a straight line.

Leg-yielding increases submissiveness to the sideways-driving aids. The leg-yield is done at the walk and later at the trot.

INSTRUCTIONS:

1. The inside rein takes a little pressure to give the horse a slight flexion to this side. The outside rein acts as a guarding rein to prevent too much flexion and to keep the horse from escaping over the outside shoulder. The outside rein gives as much as needed to flex the horse but also has the "counter pressure" to prevent overflexing. Remember: we call the "inside" the direction in which the horse is flexed, even when this side

turns toward the outside of the arena.

2. Put weight on your inside seat bone to support the inside-leg aid. Shifting your weight to the inside is supposed to make the horse not only yield to your leg aid, but shift his weight, too, so his back is suppling better.

3. Bring your inside leg back slightly into the position of a sideways-driving leg aid and push the horse forward and sideways with the rhythm of the moving hind leg.

4. Your outside leg is back in the guarding position to prevent the horse from moving more sideways than forward. While your inside leg gives the lateral direction, your outside leg encourages the horse to move forward.

MISTAKES:

If you angle the horse's hindquarters more than 45 degrees, he will only move sideways instead of the desired forward sideways, and he will lose rhythm and may even step on his own feet or turn around completely. This mistake often happens because the rider only uses the sideways driving inside leg and no or insufficient outside guarding leg. Ease the pressure on your inside leg and increase the amount of pressure with the outside

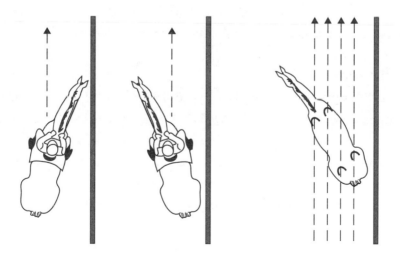

Three views of leg-yield

guarding leg. You may need to use the outside rein more strongly, leading the horse's forehand more into the direction of the motion. In addition, check if your inside-rein pressure may be too strong.

Some riders try to leg-yield by mainly pulling strongly on the inside rein in combination with insufficient outside rein and inside leg. The horse gets way overflexed, his whole neck pulled over to the side, and does not move in balance anymore. He drifts away over the outside shoulder, starts to rush forward, and won't leg-yield. Use the outside rein more to keep the horse's neck from overflexing.

Many riders fall forward in the upper body during the leg-yield or lean to the side of the sideways-driving leg and then eventually collapse in the upper body. Use the arena mirrors to observe your position.

With the inexperienced rider, the horse may only cross over with the front legs and cheat behind, moving forward only instead of sideways. Or, he continues moving straight, completely ignoring the rider's commands. Drive more strongly with the inside leg and tap the horse with a crop each step to intensify the leg aid.

Some horses rush forward to escape the aids, often falling into a trot. Shorten the reins to slow the horse down. The opposite reaction is the horse refusing to cooperate by slowing or stopping. Insist with your aids that the horse keep moving.

TRAINING TIPS:

In the very beginning, ride the leg-yield along the wall of the arena's long side, pushing sideways with the leg that is on the side of the wall and the horse flexed toward it. This way, the horse has a visual border that gives you the opportunity to concentrate on your aids without using too much rein aid in case the horse wants to escape the movement by going forward. Later ride without a wall and rely only on your aids. You do this by turning the horse toward the inside of the arena or on the centerlines or quarterlines. Finish the leg-yield and straighten the horse before you ride into a corner.

Leg-yielding is an excellent first way to teach sideways-driving aids to the rider. It also teaches the rider to combine various leg, weight, and rein aids. While learning to leg-yield, try to feel how your body aids must inter-act and flow with each other to achieve the movement. Whenever we for-get one aid or apply it too intensely, the horse will react. Leg-yield, as the first lateral motion the rider is introduced to, will be one of the most diffi-cult things to learn as a beginner.

A variation is the leg-yield on the line of a circle with the horse's fore-hand turned into it, preferably on the open side of the circle or on a slight-ly decreased circle line.

LEG-YIELDING IN A ZIGZAG AT THE LONG SIDE OF THE ARENA

This is also called "decreasing and enlarging the arena in a leg-yield," a translation of the German term *Viereck verkleinern und vergroessern*. This vari-ation of leg-yielding asks for more precise aids of the rider and submissive-ness of the horse. The horse moves in a leg-yield forward and sideways par-allel to the long side on two diagonal lines of about the figure of a single loop.

Start from a changing point (K,H,F, or M) and ride forward and side-ways on a diagonal line toward the center of the arena (being 5 meters away from the wall at B/E in a 40-meter arena, riding to X in the 60-meter arena). Return forward and sideways on a diagonal line back to the chang-ing point at the end of the long side.

INSTRUCTIONS:

1. After riding through the corner, change the horse's flexion. Start the aids for the leg-yield at the changing point. The horse's body should stay parallel to the wall. The quarters should not advance the forehand.

2. Reaching the quarter/centerline give up the flexion, ride the horse straight for about one-horse length, and then flex him to the other side to move back toward the changing point.

The movement is ridden at the walk and the trot after horse and rider have learned leg-yielding along the long sides of the arena.

TRAINING TIPS:

Zigzag leg-yield is an excellent preparation for the later half-pass and

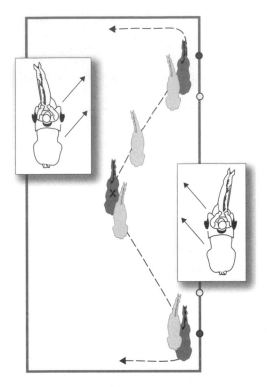

Leg-yielding in a zigzag

zigzag half-passes. When the horse is secure in the leg-yield in trot, start changing the flexion into the one for half-pass, toward the direction of the motion for brief periods. Switching from leg-yield to half-pass flexion supples the horse in the neck muscles and increases submissiveness.

SIMPLE CHANGE OF LEAD IN THE CANTER

We also call the simple change of lead in the canter a simple change of leg in the canter. This is, for example, changing from a left-lead canter to a right-lead canter by riding a transition from the left-lead canter into the walk, then walking for three to five strides before transitioning into the right-lead canter. Both transitions must show no trot in between. The walk strides must be in a secure rhythm. The rider prepares the horse before both transitions with half halts.

In lower levels we ride the simple change of lead when changing rein, so we are always cantering on the true lead. We ride the change at the point of the changing figure where the new lead begins or shortly before this point. For example, changing rein from circle to circle, we start the down transition to the walk shortly before X. Then we depart in the new canter shortly after X. On figures like the diagonal or centerline, we can ride the change of lead somewhere on the straight line, whenever desired, or whenever commanded. In advanced levels, we ride changes of lead from a true to a counter canter or vice versa.

TRAINING TIPS:

Temperamental horses tend to jig instead of clearly walk between canters because they anticipate the next depart and lack the calmness to stay in a walk. In training, vary the length of walk between down transitions and depart from the one horse length to whole rounds, going large or circling to distract the horse, regain a clear walk, and get rid of his over-eagerness. Also vary the places where you do a simple change so the horse cannot anticipate that easily. During the walk phase, relax so you do not anticipate the depart too much and contract part of your body, which causes the horse to do the same.

COUNTER CANTER

Riding a left-lead canter on the right lead or vice versa on the left lead is counter canter. It is the classical exercise, in addition to the shoulder-in, to collect and straighten a horse. Before introducing counter canter, the horse must be sufficiently secure, balanced, and in rhythm in the working canter and able to do slightly collected strides.

You can achieve the necessary amount of beginning collection with the following exercises: working canter going large and on the circle, riding transitions in the pace (extension toward a free working canter or medium canter). In the down transitions you shorten the strides from working to collected canter. The horse now learns to canter with strides of different lengths.

INSTRUCTIONS:

1. Ride counter canter with the usual canter aids. Flexion and bend stay the same, meaning the horse is flexed and bent to the left in the left-lead counter canter, although the left is on the outside of the arena.

2. You have weight on the inside seat bone with the inside hip moved forward a little.

3. The outside guarding leg is very important, as it helps keep the horse straight and in the canter.

4. The inside rein keeps the horse flexed at all times but must be soft enough to allow the inside legs to move forward.

MISTAKES:

Some riders hold too strongly with the inside rein, unbalancing the horse. The horse might break to the trot or get faster and more unbalanced because of too much weight on his outside shoulder. The outside rein controls the outside shoulder and keeps it in to straighten the horse.

TRAINING TIPS:

Introduce counter canter to the horse using the following exercises:

• The horse should know simple changes of lead in the canter and be able to execute walk-canter, canter-walk transitions. Depart into a counter canter from the walk while you are on the long side of the arena. Ride counter canter along the long side, transitioning into the walk before you reach the corner. Do this exercise on the first and second track. You can either walk the short side or ride a true canter there. After some training, start passing through shallow corners and along short sides in the counter canter. Always be satisfied with little in the beginning. Consider it a success when the horse stays in a counter canter at all during a corner. Frequent simple changes using the counter canter will help increase concentration, submissiveness, and collection.

• Riding canter, do a half volte with change of rein in the corner at the end of the arena's long side. You want to arrive rather late, coming toward the first track in a flat angle. This makes it easier for the horse in the beginning. The first few times, ride a down transition from the counter canter before you reach the corner of the short side. Later, ride through the corner, but still ride shallow corners to make it easier.

Riding the corners, the rider keeps the horse's flexion (toward the arena wall) and uses his outside guarding leg to support the horse sufficiently and not lose the counter canter.

• Riding canter, do a change of rein on the short diagonal. You work as in the previous exercise, arriving in a flat angle at the wall to make balancing easier for the horse.

You must not perform the two figures identically; to the contrary, slightly changing them to have appropriate conditions for the horse to learn the counter canter is recommended. You can also ride a mixture of both figures.

It may take quite awhile before the horse feels comfortable with counter canter. Some horses have been taught that counter canter is "wrong" and not wanted by the rider (that is why you should only correct, not punish, a "false" counter canter in the young horse. Punishment creates a bad memory). Work counter canter evenly on both leads.

When the horse is secure and comfortable with counter canter, straighten the horse more. Bringing the forehand in front of the hindquarters, riding in a travers-like angle, and riding circles and voltes in counter canter will make the horse elastic and straight. Transitions in the canter paces will increase collection.

PIROUETTES

In a pirouette the horse's forehand makes a half or full circle around the hind legs, which are also moving on a very small circle. We ride pirouettes in walk or canter. The half-pirouette is a turn of 180 degrees; the full pirouette is a turn of 360 degrees.

Half-pirouette in walk between two halts/turn on the haunches

The turn on the haunches begins with a halt and is ridden in the walk. Flexed and slightly bent toward the direction of the turn, the horse's forehand moves around the hind legs 180 degrees, a half circle.

The hind legs also move on a very small circle with the pivot point as close as possible to the inside hind foot. The front legs step forward and sideways and cross each other, while the hind legs do not cross. The inside hind leg moves up and down within the sequence of walk. The outside hind leg makes a half circle as small as possible around the inside hind. During the movement, the horse leaves the track toward the inside of the arena for about a horse's width. To bring the horse back to the track you began on, ride the last step sideways and forward. At this point the outside hind leg can cross the inside. The movement ends with a halt.

INSTRUCTIONS:

1. In the halt, shift your weight more to your inside seat bone and flex the horse in the direction of the motion.

2. Use the inside rein to flex the horse and lead the forehand into the turn. Use the outside rein to guard the amount of flexion (acting as counter pressure to the action of the inside rein to keep the horse framed) but with enough softness to allow movement in the direction of the leading inside rein.

3. Keep your inside leg in the forward-driving position and your outside leg in the guarding position. Both legs bend the horse and command his hind legs to move rhythmically and actively, engaging them to move slightly forward underneath the center of gravity. Your inside leg prevents the inside hind from escaping sideways. Your outside leg maintains forwardness during the movement. (If you push sideways with the outside leg, you will force the horse's hind legs to cross and his inside hind to escape toward the inside.)

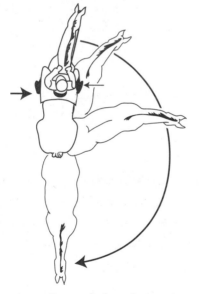

Turn on the haunches

4. Both legs initiate the motion, while the inside rein leads the forehand around. The outside rein cues rhythmically. The last one or two steps lead and push the horse sideways and forward back to the original track. After finishing the turn, stop and straighten the horse to a square halt.

TRAINING TIPS:

It is easier for the beginning rider and horse to start the pirouette with one or two steps forward before switching into the lateral movement. This will prevent the rider from using too much rein aid and the horse from avoiding the rider's aids by stepping backward or pivoting his inside hind foot in one spot. Stepping back or pivoting with the inside hind ("glued inside hind foot") are judged as bigger mistakes than a pirouette that is too large because of too much forward motion.

The walk pirouette is a collecting movement, therefore requiring secure handling of the aids. The advanced rider may be able to attempt it during the lower training stages (purposely riding the pirouette extra large to make it easier). The less-trained rider should learn to use the lateral aids before trying the pirouette with a horse not yet trained to do it. With a higher-trained horse, the less-trained rider can try out the feeling and learn from this schoolmaster.

When both horse and rider are inexperienced with a turn on the haunches, the movement may not work at all at the beginning, which can lead to much frustration. The rider is not able to coordinate his aids in a way that helps the horse turn around his haunches. An uncom-

In the walk pirouette...

the horse's forehand...

makes a circle around the hind legs

mon approach can help here. Start from the walk rather than a halt. Give all aids for a leg-yield without flexing the horse toward the sideways-driving leg. When the horse moves the first steps sideways, restrain the forward motion on the rein of the side of the sideways-driving leg. The other rein leads into the direction of the pirouette turn. If this works for several steps, switch to giving the horse the correct flexion, and use your aids so he will not cross the hind legs anymore. This gives you a start in turning the forehand around the hind legs. (As noted in the tips below, we are not, according to classical theory, supposed to compare a pirouette to a leg-yield, but this mainly mental different approach helps immensely in real life.)

Half-pirouette in walk

Ride the half-pirouette in walk the same way as above without halting before or after. To prepare for the pirouette from the walk, slightly collect the horse in the last steps by giving several half halts.

MISTAKES:

When your aids are disorganized, your weight might shift accidentally on the outside seat bone and you may not apply enough sideways-leading inside rein. You may hold back too strongly with the outside guarding rein and your outside leg may push too strongly in a lateral manner (you may mistakenly think of the pirouette as a lateral movement like the leg-yield). Your inside leg may not keep contact or pressure at all.

These errors will make the horse move around like a boat — the front end goes in the opposite direction of the rear end. The pivoting point moves toward the center of the horse in what is sometimes called "turn on center," which is wrong.

Imagine, instead, turning the horse around like a boat with its stern tied to a pole by a rope just a few inches long. To make the turn, you need to move the front end around while the stern can only move on the little space the rope gives. The outside rein holds the horse back just enough to change from a forward motion to a forward and sideways one. The inside rein leads the way with softly vibrating cues. In the beginning you can almost move both hands into the direction of the turn to make the horse understand. All your aids, both reins, both legs, and the weight shifted on your inside seat bone frame the horse and lead the way into the turn. The outside leg holds on with enough pressure to show direction, while the inside leg gives soft pressure to keep the horse's inside hind leg in place and moving. Be aware that you still have the left-right left-right counter-action in your leg pressure that you have in a walk.

TRAINING TIPS:

Making the turn extra large in the beginning of training is easier for the horse and prevents the hind feet from getting immobile, or "glued to the ground." Whenever you do the pirouette as small as is correct and the "gluing" of the hind feet occurs, go back to a larger turn while using your leg aids more actively. If the "gluing" only happens sometimes while the movement is still new to the horse, but he did the turn exceptionally well and seems to understand and obey the movement, keep working like this for a while so the horse understands before making everything absolutely correct. Sometimes you have to be content with only partially correct new movements in order to reward your horse for understanding and learning.

Riding the pirouette for too long may result in the horse coming behind the bit and the rider's aids, losing impulsion to move forward. Try not to do too much at a time, and move the horse forward energetically in trot or canter right after finishing.

If the horse does the turn with hurried steps and rushes through the movement, use inside-leg pressure and an outside rein to slow him down. A good cure is riding only a few steps of the turn at a time, for example only 90 degrees, then proceed straight ahead immediately. After a while the horse will react to the rider's inside-leg aid to slow it down.

LATERAL MOVEMENTS

All lateral movements increase the horse's submissiveness to all aids and improve flexion, bend, and balance. They gymnasticize the hindquarters and create collection by developing the carrying power of the quarters.

Correctly used lateral movements improve the gaits and length of stride.

We divide lateral movements into two groups. The first are those movements in which the horse is worked on four tracks and the front and hind legs cross each other. We position the horse in a bigger angle, about 45 degrees, and flex to the opposite side of the direction of the movement. The horse is flexed in head and neck but not bent in his longitudinal axis. Leg-yielding in its different variations belongs to this group, and partly the turn on the forehand, as it is a preparation for sideways-driving aids and involves the crossing of the legs. We use these movements to introduce rider and horse to sideways-driving aids. Once learned, you can perform them during the warm-up phase to achieve more suppleness of the horse. The crossing hind legs create an intense up and down motion of the horse's hips, which spreads to his back and has a suppling effect.

The second group is the shoulder-in, travers, renvers, and the half-pass. We position the horse at a smaller angle and on only three tracks. Head and neck are flexed in the direction of the movement, and we bend the horse in his longitudinal axis. The current hind leg is not crossing over the other hind but driven in the direction of the diagonal front leg and therefore toward the center of gravity. The lateral movements develop the straightening of the horse and equal elasticity and reactions on both leads. The smaller angle of fore- and hind legs, which brings the hind legs toward the center of gravity instead of crossing each other, makes these movements collected.

Angling the horse too much results in disturbances of rhythm and balance and loss of control of the outside shoulder. We mainly ride these lateral movements in trot and canter. Doing them in walk can make the horse understand the aids in the beginning. As these movements require a greater amount of concentration and collection, we work them only briefly. Interrupt by riding straight lines to check the desired result: increased collection. Extend to medium gaits to check the increased impulsion and maintain the forward impulse.

RIDING "IN FLEXION"/SHOULDER-FORE

These are exercises to prepare the horse for the shoulder-in and other lateral movements. You can use them at earlier training stages as they are easier for horse and rider than the other lateral movements. Shoulder-fore and, later, shoulder-in improve the horse's straightness because they ask the horse's inside hind leg to follow the inside front leg, thus carrying more weight. The rider encourages the outside hind leg of the horse to step forward in the direction between the front legs. This makes the horse track smaller with the hind legs.

You ride in flexion on the arena's long sides, meaning instead of keeping the horse straight on the straight line, you flex him slightly to the inside. In the shoulder-fore we flex the horse toward the inside and bring the forehand toward the inside, too, but not as much as in the shoulder-in.

SHOULDER-IN

In this movement, we move the horse's forehand off the track of the outside hind leg enough that the outside shoulder is in front of the inside hip. The inside hind leg steps toward the outside front leg. Watching from the front you see three tracks. On the outside track the outside hind leg is moving forward; on the middle track the inside hind leg and the outside front leg move together; on the inside track the inside front moves forward.

The horse is flexed opposite the direction of the movement and bent in the longitudinal axis as much as anatomically possible. The increased amount of bend of the haunches develops collection and elasticity, which again improve the horse's straightness. The movement mainly influences the inside hind leg to carry more weight and swing toward the center of gravity.

INSTRUCTIONS:

1. The inside rein asks for flexion and bend, while the outside rein maintains pressure to guard the horse's outside shoulder. Rhythmically given half halts on the outside rein regulate pace and rhythm and the amount of flexion.

2. The inside leg stays in the forward-driving position to engage the

Shoulder-in

horse's inside hind leg to step forward underneath the weight and to bend the horse's body.

3. The outside leg in the guarding position prevents the hindquarters from escaping toward the outside and this way keeps the hind legs moving close beside each other.

4. Shift your weight more on the inside seat bone.

5. The rider's hips and shoulders stay parallel to the horse's shoulders. This prevents collapsing to the inside, which is undesired and would shift weight and buttocks toward the outside.

Starting the shoulder-in just after the corner on the long side can make executing the movement easier because you still have flexion and bend established.

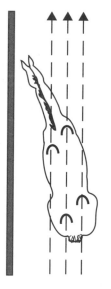

Shoulder-in

MISTAKES:

A too strongly used inside rein will flex the horse too much, forcing the horse to escape over the outside shoulder, eventually bringing him on four instead of three tracks. The inside leg pushing strongly sideways can also cause moving on four tracks. If the horse comes behind the bit and irregularities of rhythm occur, ride straight lines immediately and do extensions of the gait to regain impulsion and rhythm. Some horses tend to tilt their head, especially to the right, the right ear coming lower than the left and the mouth twisted toward the left. To correct this, push more actively and lead with a higher inside fist.

TRAVERS/QUARTERS-IN

Similar to the shoulder-in, in the travers the inside hind leg is gymnasticized more. We move the horse's hindquarters toward the second track, while the forehand stays on the first track. This brings the outside hip of the horse almost behind the inside shoulder. Watching from the front, we have the following three visible tracks: on the outside the outside front leg, in the middle the outside hind and the inside front, on the inside track the inside hind leg. The horse is flexed and bent in the direction he is moving. The inside hind leg steps forward underneath the center of gravity, carrying the most weight, and his haunches are more strongly bent.

INSTRUCTIONS:

1. Begin past the corner at the long side of the arena after you have straightened the horse. Shift your weight slightly onto the inside seat bone.

2. Using your outside leg as a guarding and sideways-pushing aid, move the horse's hindquarters toward the inside of the arena so that the outside hind leg comes into the track of the inside front. The outside leg maintains the lateral motion.

3. Keep your inside leg at the girth in the forward-driving position to engage the horse's inside hind leg to step forward underneath the center of gravity. It also creates and keeps the bend in the longitudinal axis together with the inside rein. By activating the horse's inside hind leg, your

Travers

inside leg will achieve collection.

4. The inside rein flexes head and neck, supporting the inside leg in giving the bend and the outside leg in keeping the lateral motion.

5. The outside rein has the counteracting role of allowing the flexion and bend and regulating rhythm by controlling the outside shoulder.

6. Before reaching a corner, the forehand is turned in front of the quarters. The horse is moved over to the first track with outside rein and inside -leg aid, keeping the inside flexion.

MISTAKES:

When the horse is overbent in neck and shoulder, his body is not bent evenly in its length and he moves his quarters too far toward the inside, resulting in four instead of three tracks. The outside legs will cross the inside ones, disturbing the rhythm of pace and causing the inside hind leg to escape sideways instead of carrying more weight. A stronger outside rein and inside leg can correct this by keeping the horse on three tracks only. The common mistake in the rider's seat is having the stronger weight on the outside seat bone provoked by the actively working outside leg.

TRAINING TIPS:

We ride travers mainly in collected trot or canter. As with the shoulder-in, we ride it in walk only in the beginning to help the horse understand the movement. When starting the travers as a new movement, it is helpful to use the inside flexion and bend that the horse already has going through the corner and begin the travers right after the corner without straightening.

RENVERS/QUARTERS-OUT

In the renvers, the horse's forehand is moved toward the inside of the arena like in the shoulder-in, but, in this case, we flex and bend into the direction of motion. We see three tracks again. On the track beside the arena wall is the inside hind leg. (Remember: the inside is always the direction in which the horse is bent.) In the center track is the outside hind and the inside front. On the inside track is the outside front leg.

Travers

INSTRUCTIONS:

1. Coming out of the corner onto the long side, flex and bend the horse toward the wall.

2. With your new inside leg and outside rein move the forehand toward the inside of the arena until the horse's inside front leg is in front of the outside hind.

3. Your outside leg keeps the horse's quarters at the wall, maintains the bend of his body, and prevents his outside hind leg from escaping toward the side. The inside rein keeps flexion and bend.

4. Your inside leg only pushes as much as necessary to keep the horse's hind leg engaged and stepping in the direction of the center of gravity.

5. Keep your weight on the inside seat bone. Your hips should be parallel to the horse's hips, and your shoulders parallel to the horse's shoulders. To do this you need to move your outside shoulder forward.

6. To end the renvers use both legs to push and the inside rein to bring the horse's forehand back toward the wall and in front of his hindquarters.

TRAINING TIPS:

Renvers is mostly used in the collected trot, but it can be done in walk and canter, too. Teaching the horse the renvers, the following combination of movements is very helpful: ride shoulder-in on the long side up to the changing point at the end. Do a turn on the haunches in walk and use the flexion the horse achieved in the turn to start trot and a renvers. The most common mistake again is moving the horse too much toward the side, meaning bringing the forehand in too far.

HALF-PASS

In a half-pass, the horse is moving forward and to the side on diagonal lines in the arena, in contrast to the lateral movements travers and renvers, in which the horse moves forward-sideways on a straight line. This forward and sideways motion can move toward the inside of the arena, back to the outside, or be done in zigzag lines, mostly started from the centerline. Therefore, the zigzag half-pass is just a half-pass on previously determined lines. Riding the half-pass in a zigzag asks for increased elasticity and obedience.

The horse is ridden as in the travers, flexed and bent toward the direction of motion. The longitudinal axis is always parallel to the arena walls. The horse's forehand, smaller by nature, is slightly in front of the hindquarters to keep the horse parallel. The quarters should never be in front. The rider's aids are the same as in travers. It is helpful to start the half-pass with a few steps in shoulder-in to ensure that the forehand moves laterally first. The horse's inside front leg should do the first step of the lateral motion.

INSTRUCTIONS:

We ride half-pass mainly in collected trot and canter. During the early training of half-pass, you only ride in one direction at a time and proceed to zigzags later in training when a single half-pass is secure. When changing the direction of the lateral movement in the zigzag, we must first straighten the horse for one to three steps in walk and trot or two canter strides before we flex and bend into the new direction.

MISTAKES:

Often the rider causes the forehand to move insufficiently in front of the quarters with a too strong outside leg. Lessen your outside leg pressure, keep more pressure with your inside leg, and use your inside rein to lead the horse's head, neck, and forehand more forward. If the problem persists, think and ride as if you want to change your movement from a half-pass to riding straight on the diagonal line. Doing this you must bring the horse's head and forehand more forward. Before you have the horse straightened, apply the aids for half-pass again. The forehand definitely will be leading now.

Often horse and rider start out the movement with the hindquarters already leading. Ride a shoulder-in for several steps before changing into the half-pass.

When changing direction in a zigzag half-pass, the horse is not straightened before being flexed again and bent. Disturbances in rhythm, tilting in the poll, and loss of fluent motion occur. To correct these and improve the half-pass, frequent change into straight lines, voltes, different lateral movements, and extensions in the current gait help.

The most common fault in the rider's seat is an incorrect shifting of the weight on the outside seat bone because the rider stays behind the motion or sits more strongly on the side of the guarding/sideways-driving leg. This

Half-pass...   to the left

causes the rider to collapse to the inside. Shift your inside hip distinctly forward to help your weight stay easier on the inside seat bone and do not let your inside shoulder drop.

The horse is very tense, especially in the poll and neck area. Ride down the diagonal, switching between riding the horse in a half-pass flexion and a leg-yield flexion. Most horses loosen up in their muscles much faster this way.

TRAINING TIPS:

Switch between pushing the horse more or less sideways. If he resists the sideways-driving leg, increase the lateral motion. If the horse rushes sideways, losing rhythm and suppleness, use more inside leg and ride more forward than sideways.

Half-pass

Introduce half-pass to the horse by riding leg-yield on the diagonal. Then use your aids so that the horse stays straight in head and neck instead of the leg-yield flexion. If this works, try to change to the half-pass flexion. Another possibility is starting out from a travers, where we already have the correct flexion and bend, and adding more outside leg.

FLYING CHANGE OF LEAD IN THE CANTER

The flying change is going from a left-lead canter to a right-lead canter or vice versa while the horse remains in the gait. The change occurs during the moment of suspension that exists between two canter strides. The flying change is an advanced movement and therefore can only be taught when the horse is performing the true and the counter canter with the slightest of aids, being balanced, supple, straight, and able to collect.

From fourth level on, we ride several flying changes in a row with a pre-determined number of strides in between. These are the flying changes at pre-determined intervals, with either two, three, or four strides between changes.

The ultimate is the flying change at every stride (one tempi changes) with no canter stride in between. Presupposition for those is the perfect single flying change of leg at any predetermined place.

INSTRUCTIONS:

1. Prepare with half halts to gain more collection and attention.

2. Several strides before you take up stronger contact on the new outside rein (until now, the inside rein), soften contact on the new inside rein.

3. One canter stride before the change, start to change the horse's flexion to the direction of the new canter.

4. The new outside leg moves back into guarding position, while the former outside (new inside) leg remains a moment longer in its still guarding position.

5. The leg then shifts forward into the forward-driving position to engage the new inside hind leg of the horse to move forward energetically. Having both legs back in the guarding position will keep the horse straight, supported by the new outside rein.

6. The rider supports his leg aids by putting more weight on the new inside seat bone.

7. You must give the aid to change when the horse's outside front leg leaves the ground into the suspension.

MISTAKES:

A major mistake is visibly twisting in the hips and throwing the upper body sideways. In the change's last moment, release the new inside rein slightly. This allows the horse's inside front leg to move forward freely.

When mistakes occur such as not simultaneously changing front and hind legs, incomplete changing of the legs, or crookedness, the rider must check his seat and aids. The aids have to be timed and precise; the upper body remains still with weight aids invisible. The following will help correct changes:

• Increase the canter pace so the horse moves more freely and engages forward. Come back to more collection only when the changes improve.

• New outside rein and leg have to be the main influence to ride the change. We keep more contact on the new outside rein to get pressure off the new inside rein, which will allow the horse to change.

• The major influencing new outside leg pushes more strongly.

• Check yourself for mistakes in seat and influence, such as standing up in the saddle, weight aids given to the wrong side, bad timing, and hands holding back.

• When the hind legs change too late: use the new inside leg more strongly, shift new inside hip stronger forward, use all aids more firmly, and extend to working canter to ride the change, or ride change over ground pole.

• When the horse throws up the hindquarters in the change, perform exercises that improve suppleness and submissiveness. Then return doing the flying changes, engaging the hind legs more in order to bend the haunches more. Lighten all the aids and work on an absolutely rhythmic canter. Extend the pace right before doing a change; extend between changes.

• When the horse loses rhythm, check your rein aids to make sure your hand aids aren't too strong. Use more giving than taking rein aid during the change. Use all aids more firmly. Extend slightly before the flying change. Do more straightening exercises in between changes when the horse has become a little crooked. Use a ground pole.

TRAINING TIPS:

The flying change is a very difficult and delicate movement for the horse to learn. For this reason, we only do a few flying changes during each training session. Having these at the end of the session will give the rider sufficient time to prepare the horse for the change, and reward the horse right afterward by ending the work. Most horses will do the flying change from the right to the left easier, which should be remembered when training them.

Some possibilities on teaching the flying change:

• Change on the long or short diagonal; ride the change when coming toward the wall.

• Ride a half circle with change of rein in a corner, doing the last strides toward the wall in travers and executing the change shortly before the wall.

• Ride counter canter on a 20-meter circle, changing on the circle's open side coming toward the wall.

• Ride counter canter down the long side, doing the change when reaching the corner.

• Ride serpentines, changing canter when crossing the centerline. The flexed and bent horse can be controlled very well and often gets the idea to change very quickly. Give the impulse to change while the horse is straight (between old and new flexion).

• Ride canter on a 20-meter circle, doing the flying change when changing from circle to circle.

When horses have real difficulty learning the flying change, it is often best to train them by riding them faster during trail rides. A second possibility is cantering over a pole lying on the diagonal close to the wall of the new lead. Place the pole in a 90-degree angle to the direction of motion or at the long side in a 45-degree angle to the arena wall. The horse can anticipate the change of lead and will do the flying change when moving over the pole. Give the impulse to change while the horse canters over the pole. Then the horse understands the new task.

When a correct flying change is established, we can ride it in various places. A common occurrence while teaching the flying change is that the horse gets excited and starts to hurry and run because he loses balance. To calm the horse, the rider turns on a circle, letting the horse stretch forward-downward on the bit, then takes the reins up right after. If a loss of collection or straightening occurs, ride counter canter between changes.

CANTER PIROUETTE

In a canter pirouette, the horse's forehand makes a half or full circle around the hind legs. The inside hind leg carries more weight, bending strongly. The canter's three-beat rhythm must remain clear. We perform the canter pirouette in collection.

The half-pirouette consists of three to four canter strides, the full pirouette six to eight strides. You must take enough canter strides to maintain cadence and balance. Generally, the horse does two canter strides for a quarter turn (90 degrees).

INSTRUCTIONS:

The rider prepares the pirouette by increasing collection to achieve more cadence and slow the pace.

1. The inside leg pushes more strongly to keep the three-beat rhythm and prevent the horse's hindquarters from moving travers-like.

2. The inside rein gives clear flexion and shows the direction of motion. If the horse still moves the haunches, the rider employs a shoulder-fore.

3. The outside rein keeps the flexion, giving half halts to keep the horse's hind legs on a small circle. Both rein aids must be soft enough not to disturb the fluency of motion.

4. The outside leg is in guarding position to bend the horse around the inside leg, keep the sideways motion, and to prevent the horse's outside hind leg from moving away from the weight.

5. The rider's shoulders stay parallel to the horse's, his hips parallel to the horse's hips.

6. Ending the pirouette, the rider's outside rein and driving inside leg lead the horse onto a straight line again. Actively forward-driving legs restore any lost impulsion.

MISTAKES:

• The rider leans into the direction of motion or collapses to this side. This happens often because the rider exaggerates the inside weight aid.

• The rider moves one or both hands too far over in the direction of motion. This makes the horse tilt in the poll.

Common escapes of the horse:

• His hind legs escape to the outside. Use the guarding outside leg and outside rein more.

• He loses impulsion.

• The horse is balanced incorrectly with too much weight on the inside front leg. Use all aids to regain more impulsion and straightening. When necessary, quit the pirouette for a moment to ride straight forward and extend the canter several times.

• The horse loses bend and flexion. The inside rein and leg must exert more influence; the outside leg assists to keep bend in longitudinal axis.

TRAINING TIPS:

Increase collection and bring the horse's outside hind leg sufficiently underneath the center of gravity.

Introducing the pirouette to the horse, we ride the movement "decreasing of a circle." When the horse is able to collect and balance on this small circle, we start riding travers on this line. From the travers-like canter, we guide the horse into a few pirouettes, a few strides at a time. Always ride the horse forward in between and extend the canter to restore impulsion,

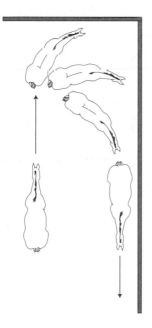

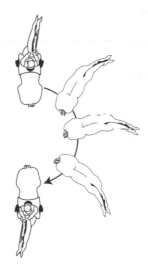

Introduction to the canter pirouette   Canter pirouette

balance, and straightness.

Another possibility is using the arena walls as helpers. Ride counter canter on the quarterline along the long side so you have approximately two-horse-lengths distance to the wall. Before you reach the short side, turn toward the wall to do a half-pirouette. In the beginning the turn is a small reverse volte; later the horse will do the pirouette. The arena wall builds a natural restriction and prevents the horse from going too large.

Training canter pirouettes, we ride on circles with a far bigger diameter than we want to ride the perfected pirouette on. Canter pirouette puts great stress on the horse's hindquarters, even for a highly trained and conditioned horse. So, during most training sessions we work the horse in a "working pirouette," in which we let the hind legs make a bigger circle of about 2 meters. This will prevent the horse from being harmed.

HALF STEPS

Half steps are collecting the horse in half trot steps. We engage the horse to do extremely shortened but highly collected trot steps. The horse hardly covers any ground but is greatly bent in the haunches, so the main motion goes energetically up and down, not forward. The moment of suspension is prolonged. This highly collecting movement prepares for the piaffe and passage. We can introduce them during higher levels to improve collection and increase the bend of the haunches.

INSTRUCTIONS:

1. Start half steps from a slightly shortened walk, halt, or collected trot. Starting from the walk is preferred, as there is less chance that you will act too strongly with your hands. Often it is easier to start on bent lines such as a big volte, where controlling the horse is easier.

2. With a slightly braced spine, weight on both seat bones, and both legs driving forward into taking and giving reins, push the horse into half trot steps.

3. Repeatedly given half halts will encourage the hind legs to bend in the haunches and step underneath the center of gravity. Extremely rhyth-

mic application of the aids is very important. Do not hold a single half halt for longer than one step.

4. End the half steps with a square halt or by transitioning into an extended trot, which helps regain forwardness and impulsion.

EXERCISE COMBINATIONS

You will find some of the following combinations of movements useful to improve certain aspects of training. These are just a few ideas to combine movements to achieve progress in training. Many more possibilities exist.

Riding with counter flexion

Riding the horse with counter flexion means we flex and bend the horse to the outside instead of the inside. We can do this in all gaits and paces, introducing it in walk first to give the horse time to get used to it. Counter flexion increases the horse's concentration and submissiveness, helps straighten him, and corrects the horse's preferred drifting to the outside. Riding with counter flexion works as a preparation for the counter canter and the lateral movements.

Start with riding walk in counter flexion in corners and on the circle. You first only flex the horse in the neck, then later bend the horse's body. When the horse gets accustomed to this, use counter flexion in trot and canter. Ride in counter flexion in shortened or collected gaits.

Counter flexion especially on a circle is an excellent method to let the rider experience his ability to apply his outside aids and to frame the horse between inside and outside. Switching to counter flexion, the horse's inside changes. If the rider does not sufficiently guard the horse with the outside aids (to the circle inside), his hindquarters will drift into the circle. The importance of guarding outside aids becomes much more obvious to the rider than when a horse drifts toward the arena outside.

Extended trot/walk pirouette/extended trot

Extend the trot along the long side of the arena. Transition to a walk shortly after the circle point at the end of the long side. Walk only for two to three steps at the most, then do a walk pirouette and start extended trot again immediately after finishing. Repeat this combination at the other end of the long side. This is an excellent exercise to check how well the individual movements are learned by the horse, and it improves concentration and submissiveness.

Extend the canter strides in counter canter

Ride extended canter along the long side of the arena in counter canter. This helps straighten the horse and overcome his tendency to bring the haunches in. Riding on the first track, right beside the arena wall, the horse cannot move his haunches in this direction.

Canter in shoulder-fore position

Ride in a shoulder-fore or shoulder-in position while doing canter and canter extensions. This brings the horse's forehand in front of his hindquarters so he moves straight.

Serpentines/voltes combination

Ride serpentines through the width of the arena in trot. Begin with a volte in the first corner before leaving the first track (while you are in your first loop) and then ride a volte at the center point of each loop. Stay in the volte for one round or as long as you need to bring the horse in correct flexion and bend and only then continue into the next loop. This exercise increases submissiveness, elasticity, suppleness, flexion, and bend. It also educates horses that tend to anticipate the next change of direction and drift.

Riding on the second track

Ride part of your daily training session on the second track in whatever gait or movements you are doing. This is very good education for the horse as well as the rider, as both have to be without the arena wall building a natural restriction on the outside. The horse learns to listen better to the outside aids; the rider learns to use the outside aids sufficiently.

Decreasing the circle in canter

Decrease the circle down to a volte in the canter; stay there for several rounds while applying half halts to collect the canter. The small turn will automatically collect the horse some. To finish, increase the circle again, driving the horse forward to regain possibly lost impulsion. Do walk/canter/walk transitions with a few strides only at the canter while on the volte. These exercises collect the canter and increase submissiveness.

Walk/canter/walk transitions

Transition from the walk to a canter by staying in the canter for a few strides (try to come down to two to three strides only) and then transitioning down to the walk again. Repeat this often. The first few canter strides will always be slightly collected, then balance and self-carriage lessen. Before this happens we transition down to the walk. The horse learns collected canter through frequent transitions, getting increasingly collected strides each time. Submissiveness also improves.

Improving lateral movements

Ride various lateral movements at different places in the arena, on straight as well as bend lines. These exercises improve the horse's concentration and submissiveness to your aids.

Leg-yield/partial turn on the forehand/leg-yield

This exercise improves the horse's acceptance of the lateral aids and increases his attention. Ride a leg-yield along the long side. Toward the end come to a halt, staying in the angle or about the 45 degrees you had for the leg-yield. Start a turn on the forehand and stop when you are again in a 45-degree angle to the wall. Continue walking and ride a leg-yield again.

Shoulder-in/volte/shoulder-in

Ride shoulder-in along the long side of the arena, turning into voltes at various places, and then continue the shoulder-in. This exercise lets the rider control the horse's forward motion. Another variation is riding shoulder-in, volte, and travers or vice versa.

Extending the trot from a shoulder-in

Ride this extension either staying on the long side or turning to ride diagonally across the arena to the opposite side. This gives the horse more freedom in the forehand, so impulsion and length of stride increase.

Changes between shoulder-in and travers

Ride changes between shoulder-in and travers during a long side, sometimes with a volte in between. This perfects submissiveness and obedience.

Developing half-pass from a shoulder-in

Ride shoulder-in for a short distance and then change into a half-pass, taking the clear flexion and bend over to the new movement. This helps prevent the horse's hind legs from coming in front of the forehand in the half-pass.

Improving the transition to a halt

Transitions from the trot to a halt first require the training of many transitions from a trot to a walk to improve submissiveness. Then work trot/walk/halt transitions. Shorten the number of walk steps between trot and halt every time until there are no more. The horse will be less resistant this way, have more time to balance and follow your aids, and will be able to stand square sooner.

Rein back in combination with transitions

In advanced training stages we ride the rein back in combination with transitions, such as trot/halt/rein back/trot or canter/halt/rein back/canter, called "alternated rein back/forward/rein back." These combinations develop collection and reveal how well the horse is gymnasticized and submissive. With the advanced horse you can do the "swing" instead of a simple rein back.

Half-pass/volte/half-pass

Start a half-pass on the diagonal. Around X ride a volte into the direction the horse is flexed, then proceed right away with half-pass. This exercise helps supple the horse during half-pass, improving the horse's flexion and bringing the forehand more in the lead.

11 | Dressage Terms

Classical dressage has developed its own language. These terms describe certain conditions, positions, and actions with absolute precision. Knowing "dressage language" makes possible a better and quicker understanding between dressage riders or trainer and student.

You can find the following terms in context throughout the chapters of this book.

CORRECT HEAD AND NECK POSITIONS

The following are terms for positions of the horse's head and neck at different stages and for the influence of the aids.

Position (of head and neck)

Position reflects how the horse's head and neck are situated when observed from the side, whether maintained by the rider or the horse himself and no matter whether suppleness and contact exist.

Contact

Contact is the rider's connection to the horse's mouth with the reins. The horse leans on both reins equally and as softly as possible. With true contact, the horse is submissive to all aids. It does not mean a forced shaping of the position of head and neck.

On the bit

The horse follows the commands of the rider's rein aids with willingly bent neck and poll muscles. The contact between rider's hands and the horse's mouth is soft but steady. The horse's mouth stays closed. The tongue remains underneath the bit without trying to escape the pressure of the bit. A little foam shows around the lips, resulting from a soft chewing on the bit. The horse's neck has a convex shape, rounded upward. The upper neckline describes a quarter-circle. The poll is the highest point of

On the bit

neck. The horse's noseline is one to two fingers' width in front of an imaginary vertical line. The height at which head and neck are positioned depends on the training stage of the horse. It varies from the lowest extended position of the young horse up to the elevated position of the advanced horse in collection (see below for these definitions).

The horse is on the aids

The horse is on the bit as described above. In addition, he responds willingly to the rider's back/weight and leg aids without escaping them. Engaged by the driving aids, the horse searches for the contact on the reins without pulling. He is obedient. The horse is "stepping through the poll" when these muscles are supple.

Extended head and neck position of the young horse

The head and neck position we use to ride young horses during initial training. Head and neck are in a lower and more extended frame. The horse's mouth is at the same height as the point of shoulder. The young horse's neck stretches forward more than in advanced horses. All requirements of being on the bit and on the aids stay the same. In this position, the young horse can build up muscles, condition, and strength for the higher levels without excessive demand.

Head and neck position of the horse on the way to collection

As the training level increases, the horse's head and neck position changes. The mouth is in a higher position. The neck gets shorter. This allows the horse to develop more driving and carrying power of the hindquarters.

Elevated position of the advanced horse in collection/raising of the forehand

When collection lowers the hindquarters, head and neck raise because the center of gravity of the horse changes. The horse's mouth is now at the same height as his point of hip. The neck is in a shorter frame. The exact height relates to the grade of collection. The elevated position must result from the right collecting work and not be forced. A test for correctness is to check if the horse moves in "self carriage." In all gaits the rider must be able to ride the "give and retake the reins" for a few steps. The balanced horse will retain his head and neck position.

Collection lowers the hindquarters

The classic system distinguishes between "relative elevation" and "absolute elevation." We have relative elevation when the horse raises the forehand as the result of stronger bend in the haunches, which makes the horse seem taller in the forehand. Faulty absolute elevation results from a forced influence of the rider, inflicted mainly by the rein. The horse is not in self-carriage. He is tense in the back, and the haunches are not engaged.

The horse steps through the poll

The horse is on the bit and on the aids, being completely supple in the poll muscles. When these muscles relax, the parotid gland produces more saliva, which we can observe by the horse chewing softly on the bit and developing foam around the mouth.

To ride on a long rein

The horse is on a long rein when he carries the neck naturally and has connection to the rider's hand. The reins are longer than when riding on

the bit; therefore the neck is longer. We control the poll only very carefully. We work green horses on a long rein during the introductory training
phases. We use the long rein with advanced horses for short periods to gain
relaxation and suppleness.

To give the reins completely

The rider gives so much rein that there is no connection between rider's
hand and the horse's mouth. The reins hang down completely loose.

*To give and retake the reins/*Üeberstreichen

The give and take of the reins controls the horse's self-carriage. It shows
if the horse is steady to the rider's aids. For a few steps, the rider moves
both hands forward about one to two hand widths. During this instant, we
give up any contact to the horse's mouth. Then the hand moves carefully
back into the former position. The horse's noseline may move slightly more
in front of the vertical. The general position of head and neck and the pace
must remain the same. Sometimes we do the give and retake with one rein
only to determine if the horse remains in secure contact with the other.
This would be the inside rein in general, so we check if the horse is on the
leading outside rein.

*To let the horse stretch forward-downward on the reins/*Zuegel aus der Hand kauen lassen

From the position on the bit, the rider slowly lets the reins get longer
so that the horse can stretch forward-downward. We release until the horse
is on the "long rein." The rider must keep contact on the reins at all times.
Do not give the reins so abruptly that they are loose. The rider pushes
more strongly to keep the hindquarters active. The horse should stretch so
his mouth is level with the point of shoulder. The noseline stays in front of
the vertical. The horse must keep rhythm and pace. The rider's hands move
slightly forward to be able to retake the reins softly. We finish the exercise
by retaking the reins and bringing the horse into the former position on
the bit or by releasing the reins completely.

This movement shows if the horse is securely on the aids, in rhythm,
supple, and in contact. It is a relaxing movement, as the horse can stretch

the neck muscles. You can ride it in every gait. Young horses will gain more balance with this movement. If a horse speeds up during the exercise, this signifies that he still lacks balance.

Stretching

If the horse does not stretch sufficiently or even jerks the reins out of the rider's hands, this shows that the muscles are not supple yet. The rider probably has used more restraining than driving aids. Never perform this movement for too long or you risk the horse putting too much weight on the forehand.

INCORRECT HEAD AND NECK POSITIONS

Above the bit

The noseline is too far in front of the vertical. The horse carries head and neck too high, not rounding the upper neckline but stiffening the lower neck muscles. The horse above the bit can move against the bit, too, but not necessarily. He still may be in a soft contact but does not round its back and use his back muscles. The horse is not submissive or stepping through the poll. Riding on large bent lines applying driving aids and giving and taking rein helps bring the horse on the bit.

Against the bit

The horse is in the same head and neck position as when above the bit, but strongly pulling into the reins. Going above and against the bit over longer periods will develop wrong muscles. In order to achieve a supple horse and improve contact on the reins, extend the warm-up phase. Especially use the movement "letting the horse stretch on the reins."

Behind the bit

The horse tries to escape backward with his head to avoid contact and

Against the bit

commands of the reins. The noseline is behind the vertical. The rider cannot establish contact on the reins. Driving and carrying power of the hindquarters get lost. Often this fault is combined with a "broken neck." The reason can be an extremely sensitive mouth or rein aids given too strongly.

To solve the problem, the rider first needs to regain contact. The horse needs to trust the connection to the hands again. We ride with a longer rein and ask the horse to stretch forward again. We must combine this with sufficient forward-driving aids. It is important to keep the hands low and watch very carefully for the moment that the horse starts to stretch. Helpful are lungeing and trail riding with the emphasis on driving the horse forward energetically.

Broken neck

The horse is continuously behind the vertical. This happens because the rider forced the horse into contact with strong rein aids or the horse tends to this position. The poll is not the highest point of the neck anymore but a point farther back (mostly between the third and fourth neck vertebrae). The horse is not truly on the aids. Because the upper neck muscles develop differently, it takes a long time to correct a broken neck. Here again, the horse needs to stretch more in the neck, especially the upper neckline and search for better contact. The *Zuegel aus der Hand kauen lassen* (letting the horse stretch forward-downward on the rein) is the best cure.

Lying on the bit/using the head as fifth leg

The horse is lying on the bit when he tries to find support on the reins and props his weight on them. He uses the head as the "fifth leg" and is not sufficiently active in the hindquarters. Lazy horses have a tendency to do this.

The rider must engage the hind legs more by stronger leg aids. A sensible give and take on the reins will soften the contact

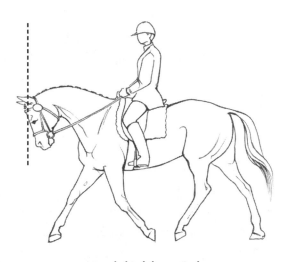

Nose behind the vertical

and does not give the horse a chance to hang onto the reins. Riding transitions will help.

Noseline behind the vertical/overbent

The horse is on the bit but with the noseline behind the vertical. Contact on the reins exists, but may be too strong. This can happen because the rider influences too strongly with the rein aids. This can come from a momentarily incorrect use of the aids or be the result of incorrect training. The hands need to soften and give more, combined with forward-driving aids.

Observing the positions behind the bit and being overbent, they look very much the same. As the overbent horse still has sufficient impulsion and carrying power of the hind legs, this is the lesser fault than behind the bit.

Tilted head (poll)

This happens when the rider flexes the horse in the neck but does not release as much on the outside rein as he takes on the inside rein. The horse receives two opposing commands from the reins and is too restricted by them. Consequently, the horse tilts his head in the poll to escape the situation. The head is not vertical anymore. The horse's ears are not on the same level. The poll tilts toward the inside (inside ear lowers), and the nose turns slightly toward the outside. To correct this, the rider straightens the horse again, giving stronger driving aids to get the horse to stretch into the reins forward-downward. Then he tries to flex again with more sensitive and clear aids. Leading with the inside hand in a slightly higher position temporarily can help, too.

OTHER TERMS

Artificial, tense steps

The horse does not put his hooves down on the ground where they point during the moment of suspension. He moves in cramp-like tension. His hind legs do not have sufficient impulsion.

Balance

Every young horse has a natural balance. His balance depends on his conformation (the proportions of body and limbs and their muscles). Natural balance differs with the individual horse. When we start to ride the horse and have our weight on his back, we disturb this natural balance. The horse needs to rebalance during training. He must learn to adjust his center of gravity with the rider on his back in all situations.

We talk about horizontal or lateral balance and vertical balance (from front to rear). Many problems or disobedience during training result from imbalance.

Bend of the body (of the horse in his longitudinal axis)

We bend the horse in his whole body, or his longitudinal axis. Longitudinal axis means the complete vertebral column from poll to tail. We bend him as much as anatomically possible. The bend should be even, so as not to have more in the neck than in the ribs.

As the horse's vertebral column is variably movable, the even bend is relative. The neck is more flexible than the back and rear of the horse. Bending the horse makes him suppler, keeps the hind legs in the track, and improves straightening. You can flex the horse in the head without bending him in his body. When you bend the horse in his longitudinal axis, you always have a flexion of the head, too.

Bending the horse, the rider puts more weight on the inside seat bone. The inside calf is pushing in the forward-driving position, engaging the inside hind leg. The outside leg is one hand's width back in the position of a guarding leg, preventing the outside hind leg from escaping to the outside. The inside rein keeps the horse flexed. The outside rein gives sufficiently to allow flexion and bend. The outside rein also restrains sufficiently to control the outside shoulder and prevent extreme bending.

The outside aids, especially the outside rein, are of great significance for the bend. The rider always flexes the horse in the head first before he bends his body. We have a maximum bend in corners and voltes, a lesser bend on all other bent lines. Bending the horse on bent lines keeps him in balance.

Bend of the haunches

The haunches consist of the hip joint, knee joint, and hock joint. The haunches create the carrying and forward-driving power of the hind legs. Bending the haunches means increasing the flexion of those joints with collected work. The hind legs will carry more weight and swing farther forward.

The extent of bending the haunches depends on the horse's conformation (*exterieur*) and willingness to work (*interieur*). Bending of the haunches creates the raising of the forehand. This looks like the horse moves "uphill." He seems taller in the front.

Bracing the spine

We brace the spine when we use our back aid. The rider contracts the muscles of belly and lower back for several strides to engage the horse's hind legs to carry more weight and step farther toward his center of gravity. While bracing the spine, we can slightly slow down or increase the rhythm in which we swing in the pelvis. The rider keeps weight on one or both seat bones. We brace the spine only for brief moments, after which we return to the normal seat position. Activating the hind legs more enables the rider to use the rein aids more softly and less often. The rider must be at a more advanced stage of training to feel and learn how to brace the spine.

It seems that the expression "bracing the back" is a direct translation of the German term *Kreuz anziehen*, which means tightening the back.

Cadence

In the collected trot, the horse gains cadence (loftiness of the strides) when he prolongs the moment of suspension with the hind legs swinging well forward.

If the moment of suspension prolongs but the hind legs do not swing sufficiently forward and the horse's back is tight, we call this "artificial or tense steps." These are incorrect because the horse is tense. You can observe this by the hooves not coming down on the ground where they point during the moment of suspension. The horse will not be supple on the aids.

Changing lead/changing rein

You change the direction you are riding in the arena using an appropriate school figure. You can change rein from the left lead to the right lead or reverse. Left lead for example means that you ride left turns in all corners. Your left side of the body shows toward the inside of the arena.

Counter flexion

We learned before that the horse's inside always is the side he is flexed to no matter if this is the inside or outside of the arena. Riding in counter flexion means riding the horse flexed and bent toward the opposite side. Exercises in counter flexion improve concentration and submissiveness. Also we can work the horse's outside hind leg more intensely and teach the horse not to "lean" toward the arena wall. We ride counter flexion only with some collection.

Flexion or bend of the head

The horse flexed or bent in the head means he turns his head to one side in the joint between head and neck. The neck must stay almost straight. With a correct and supple, flexing horse, you can observe the crest of the neck tilt toward the side of the flexion. We can keep the head straight, bent to the left or right. The longitudinal axis is not involved in this. We flex the horse to reach more submissiveness to sideways-working aids. The horse improves contact to the outside and softens on the inside aids. The side the horse is flexed to in the head is always called the "inside," the opposite side is called the "outside." This is independent from where the inside or outside of the arena might be.

To achieve flexion to one side, the rider shortens the inside rein and applies taking rein aids when necessary. The outside rein gives as much as the inside takes without losing contact. The rider keeps his weight evenly on both seat bones. With a correct flexion, the rider slightly sees the inside eye and nostril. Observed from the front, the head must remain absolutely vertical. Changing the flexion from one side to the other, we first straighten the horse briefly. Then we flex to the new direction. We give the horse flexion toward the inside on all bend lines and during many movements.

There are some very common mistakes when flexing the horse. One is holding or even pulling too much on the inside rein trying to flex, causing the neck to shorten. The inside hind leg is unable to step forward and underneath the horse's weight. If the neck is turned sideways, this causes the outside shoulder and leg to move away, resulting in gait irregularities.

Equally wrong is giving too much on the outside rein. Again we only pull the head over by the inside rein and have no control of the outside shoulder. Another fault is tilting of the head in the poll, caused by insufficient release of the outside rein (see the explanation below).

Ground cover/length of stride

The distance on the ground the horse gains with each step, the length of every single stride. We measure this by checking if the horse's hind feet step into the track of the respective front

Covering ground

leg, stay behind this point, or reach farther. How much ground cover we want depends on the pace we ride. Sufficient ground cover is a criterion for a good gait, but it can vary with the natural capability of each horse. The horse must develop more ground cover in the extended gaits and less in the collected gaits.

Lengthening of the frame/of the outline

Riding an extension in a gait, we want to see a lengthening of the frame in the horse. Observed from the side, the horse's outline gets longer during the extension. The neck stretches slightly longer. The horse's noseline moves farther forward in front of the vertical than before. The poll must still be under control. The main head and neck position stays as before. Self-carriage must remain.

Moment of suspension

In the trot and canter we have moments of suspension. This is the moment when the horse is completely off the ground with all four feet.

Natural crookedness

Every horse is born with a more or less crooked body. This "natural crookedness" describes the asymmetry of the body's left and right sides in muscle strength and elasticity. The hind legs do not extend forward into exactly the tracks of the front legs. It is comparable to the human left- or right-handedness.

The horse has, as we do, one preferred pivot and free leg. One leg is stronger and more elastic. The horse can carry better with it, and will extend this leg farther toward the center of gravity. The other, weaker hind leg extends less forward and toward the outside of the respective front leg. It does not move underneath but beside the body.

Consequently, the forehand is burdened with more weight. For example, if the horse prefers to carry with the left hind and the right hind evades toward the outside, the horse "falls" on the diagonal shoulder. The horse puts more weight on this left shoulder. He stiffens the left neck muscle, leaning too strongly on this rein; the right side of the neck gets hollow, and the horse tries to avoid contact on this rein.

You can observe crookedness for example by watching dogs at their trot. Foals show it very visibly, too. You can observe them moving very wide behind, their long legs extending forward and tracking beside the left and right of the front legs. You will rarely observe that both hind legs narrow into the track of the front leg.

Positioning the neck at the shoulder

The lesser-trained horse will always try to move his whole neck sideways, starting at the shoulder, when being flexed. This is incorrect as it brings the horse off balance. The neck of a flexed horse must be almost straight coming out off the shoulder.

We want a flexion in the poll (the second vertebrae) with only a very slight bend in the rest of the neck. So we must position or secure the neck at the shoulder. This also implies that poll and neck have a certain amount of muscle tension to be in the position of the respective training stage. This tension is elastic and functional, not cramped and disturbing.

Riding the horse in an angle

We bring the horse's forehand or hindquarter in an angle to the track it is on. We do this for all lateral movements. The amount of the angle depends on the movement and training stage of the horse.

Scale of training

The scale of training is the structure for the fundamental gymnasticizing training of the horse. It contains the six elements: rhythm, suppleness, contact, impulsion, straightening and collection. We distinguish three phases: training developing the driving power of the hind legs, and developing the carrying power of the hind legs. All of those goals require submissiveness.

Self-carriage

The horse moves in self-carriage when he is able to carry more weight with his hindquarters and the rider's weight comfortably. He keeps head and neck willingly in the desired position. The horse is balanced in all gaits. Sufficient carrying power of the hindquarters is a precondition. Then he is able to move in "self-carriage."

The check for self-carriage is the movement "give and retake the reins," or *Ueberstreichen*. Here the horse must keep position, balance, pace, and rhythm. The noseline may move slightly more in front of the vertical. The horse must remain securely on the leading outside rein and in flexion while the rider gives and retakes with the inside rein on a bend line.

Square halt

The horse stands still with equal weight on all four feet. Observed from the side, the front feet are right beside each other, as are the hind feet. A common mistake is the open position, one hind or front foot standing farther back or forward. The younger horse will not have the balance yet to do perfect square halts. A correct square halt should develop naturally through well-trained transitions, not by drilling in the halt.

The horse falls apart

The horse securely on the aids with hind legs swinging actively forward toward the center of gravity falls apart when he comes off the rider's aids. He loses impulsion, the head and neck position, and probably straightness and submissiveness. Observed from the side, the horse seems longer, as his hind legs do not move sufficiently toward the center of gravity anymore.

Appendix | Equipment for the Horse

A mericans tell me getting help finding the right saddle to fit horse and rider is very difficult. As an ill-fitting saddle can cause problems, I will discuss this subject at length. I will cover bridles and auxiliary reins only briefly.

THE SADDLE

Having the right saddle means getting the type you need for the riding you do, such as a dressage saddle for dressage riding. The right saddle fits the anatomy of the horse as well as the rider. It helps the rider sit comfortably and stay in the correct position. It fits the horse's back so well that it does not hurt and the horse has optimum freedom to move. When money is limited, buying a used brand-name saddle well known for its quality and workmanship is often better than choosing a lower-quality new saddle for the same price. Well-made saddles, given proper and regular care, will last a lifetime. When buying a saddle, new or used, do not plan to use padding to make it fit. If the saddle is to be customized for fit, make sure an expert does it, or keep looking for the right saddle. When you lack experience in saddle fitting, take somebody who has more knowledge, and make sure you try the saddle on your horse and ride in it before buying it. Although a saddle may be expertly built and of the highest quality, it will not fit every kind of horse.

The dressage saddle

The dressage saddle is made for the dressage seat only and for sitting close to the horse. It keeps the rider in an upright position, with weight on both seat bones naturally. The cantle is slightly higher than the pommel. The rear-panel cushioning should keep the rider sitting as close as possible to the horse's back. The flaps are longer than other saddle flaps because we ride with long stirrups. They are cut straight down to allow the long, almost straight leg appropriate to the dressage seat.

The dressage saddle usually has small knee rolls to help stabilize the seat but no padding behind the leg. A lot of dressage saddles have long straps with a short girth so that the straps on the tightened saddle sit below the flaps and cannot disturb the rider's calves. Today, most dressage saddles are made so well that this is not necessary. Also, the girth is easier to tighten with short straps.

Saddling the horse and care of the saddle

You put the saddle far in front of the withers when laying it on the horse, then move it slowly backward into the right position. (This way you move the saddle the same direction as the horse's hair.) The pommel should sit on the back of the withers. Usually the saddle moves into the right spot by itself. If you move the saddle back too far, lift it up again and start over so that shifting the saddle forward does not pull the hair. As most riders saddle a horse from the left, the girth stays strapped on the right side when off the horse. The girth should lie over the saddle when putting it on the horse. Also the stirrups are pulled up. If we do not get on the horse right away, the stirrups should stay pulled up. This way the horse cannot get caught somewhere and become afraid or get hurt.

On saddles with three straps on each side, the girth is attached to the same straps to evenly distribute pressure on the horse's back. Depending on the horse's anatomy, we may use the two first straps (which is very common), the first and third, or the last two to give the saddle optimum stability. Always tighten the girth hole by hole to get the horse slowly used to the pressure around his body. Check that absolutely no wrinkles or twisted hairs are underneath the girth.

Also check the stirrup leather regularly for safety. Make sure the seams are still intact. The leather where the stirrup hangs should be checked carefully so that it does not get too thin and break during riding. The stirrup bar has to open easily so that the stirrup leather can slide out in case of an accident. The stirrup should be heavy and wide enough to give the feet room and let them slide out easily in case of an accident. You can choose among the different kinds of safety stirrups on the market. Also check the straps of the saddle where you attach the girth each time.

Regular care with leather soap (consisting of oil so that it cleans but does not dry out) and grease will make your saddle and stirrup leather last longer and keep parts from breaking because of dryness.

Stirrup leathers

Intact stirrup leathers are of great importance for safety. The stirrup leathers must be of a soft yet sturdy leather of high quality. Regular care and checking for cracks or damaged seams are essential.

Stirrups

Stirrups must be sufficiently wide and heavy so the rider's foot can take or release them easily and quickly. About 4¾ inches is the proper width for adults; about 4¼ inches for children.

I would highly recommend the safety stirrups now available. In case of an accident, the foot releases from the stirrup.

COMMON CRITERIA FOR A SADDLE

Saddles vary in length; size of the tree, panel, and seat; and length of flaps.

Saddle tree and panel

Saddle trees are available in narrow, medium, and wide, depending on the height and width of the withers. For high and small withers, use a small tree so that the saddle will not sit directly on the horse's spine. For low withers (or almost none, as we find on ponies), use a wide tree so that the saddle does not sit too far above the spine.

In combination with the right tree size, we need the right type of panel (the wool-stuffed bottom of the saddle that rests on the horse's back) to fit the shape of the withers. The panel can be long or short and of different thickness. It has to be stuffed evenly so that no irregularities occur later. Even the best panel will flatten over time and require new stuffing. Uneven flattening can occur because of poor stuffing, uneven seat of the rider, or unevenly developed muscles of the horse (e.g., the young horse often has less-developed muscles in his left side, which takes training to level out). A panel stuffed too tight will flatten but meanwhile rub and bounce on the horse's back and cause pain.

The tree and the panel type and size determine the size of the channel. The channel is the open space that is supposed to keep any pressure from the horse's spine.

Length of saddle

The length of a saddle is important for the rider's position. For example, on a horse with a short back, a large saddle will press on the sensitive loin area, which can cause the horse to switch his tail, shuffle his hindquarters, or buck. On a saddle too short for the horse, the rider's weight is not distributed over enough of the horse's back.

Length of flaps, seat size

A lot of saddles are available with different flap lengths for different leg lengths. Every saddle type is available in different seat sizes to fit the different figures and weight of riders.

Fitting the saddle on the horse

For the first fitting, place the saddle on the horse's back without a saddle pad to get a better look at its fit. The horse should stand on level ground.

GUIDELINES TO FIT A SADDLE:

• Visualize a straight line parallel to the ground from the pommel to the cantle. The cantle should be slightly higher than the pommel (this can be one to three inches depending on the saddle type and brand) with the seat's deepest point in the saddle's middle. Different brands of saddles vary in construction, but almost any saddle with the cantle level with or below the pommel means the saddle is not fitting the horse.

• The saddle should have absolutely no contact with the horse's withers and spine. There should be about two fingers' clearance between the pommel and the horse's withers. This clearance extends back between the two panels to the back of the saddle so that you see a clearly visible channel from front to back. This has to be the same with the saddle girthed and the rider's weight leaning forward or backward. Make some allowance for the saddle to settle after some use.

• There should be just enough space for your hand between the pommel and withers.

• The panels on the bottom of the saddle should lie evenly along the sides of the withers from pommel to cantle and downward on the shoulders. Incomplete contact will create lateral instability, inadequate weight distribution, and discomfort for the horse.

• The panels must be stuffed correctly so that the saddle contacts the horse's back over as large of a surface as possible to distribute the weight. Panels without enough stuffing will create lumps as they settle. Panels stuffed too tight move upward in some places and therefore do not make contact with enough area.

• Panels should have sufficient stuffing so the horse's back is protected effectively but you have close contact with the horse's back. On a new saddle you may have the feeling of sitting too high above the horse's back until the panels settle.

• The saddle should not disturb the movements of the horse in any way. To check this, have someone lift up one of the horse's front legs and pull it forward, so that the horse stretches the shoulder. Now put your hand in between the upper part of the shoulder and the front part of the saddle. If this is possible, the saddle will not disturb any motion. Do this on both sides.

• The saddle should not be so long as to put pressure on the horse's back in the kidney area. To avoid weight on this sensitive part of the horse's back, be sure that the saddle does not slide onto that area while the horse is ridden.

• You should not be able to move the saddle very much from one side to the other. If you can, the saddle is not stuffed right or the panel needs to have a different shape to avoid lying too close, which will make skin and flesh sore.

• Have the saddle on the horse and stand behind it a little distance. Check if the saddle sits straight on the horse's back. Also check to see that the saddle itself is not twisted. A twisted saddle tree can be a manufacturing mistake or result from pulling yourself up with one hand at the cantle when getting on the horse. Grip the pommel or the seat to avoid this.

• From behind the horse you can also examine the condition of the back muscles. A lot of horses have less-developed muscles on one side, which will influence the fit of the saddle and probably make it seem twisted or stuffed unevenly. A new saddle may settle unevenly in the panel because of this, but can be corrected with restuffing. When the uneven development of the muscles really makes the saddle sit unevenly, change the panel stuffing right away in order to train the horse and strengthen the muscles.

• With the saddle removed, you have to be able to put a woman's fist into the channel all the way from pommel to cantle, so that air can circulate.

• When the saddle is used for several months, check the stuffing of the panels and have them restuffed when necessary.

• Whenever possible, use a saddle only for one horse. The panel can adapt to the one horse's form and the saddle will have the optimum fit.

• With used saddles, test if the saddle tree is broken (also possible with a new saddle if something happened during transport). Take hold of pommel and cantle and try to twist the saddle in different directions. There should be no twisting nor a creaking or cracking noise. The tree should be stable and not make any sound.

FITTING THE SADDLE FOR THE RIDER

Checking if a saddle fits your anatomy is easier than trying it for the horse, as you can test the saddle in the shop or at home. The most common misfits for the rider are seats that are too small, saddles that sit too high in front, and saddles in which the rise to the pommel extends too far back. For testing, you put the saddle on a "wooden horse" or the horse himself. The following points should be noted:

• Before you sit on the saddle, check if the lowest point of the seat is exactly centered between pommel and cantle. This is absolutely necessary to gain a correct position. If the lowest point is too far back, it will place the rider so that his legs automatically slide too far forward. He will have his weight too far back. If the lowest point is too far forward, the rider will lean forward with the upper body, losing the weight and back aid.

• Take a relaxed seat with loosely hanging legs and see if the saddle gives you a comfortable feeling. A brand-new saddle feels different for a few weeks because the padding still has to settle.

• A saddle has different sizes to fit different horses; it also has different sizes to fit the backside of different riders. Fit one hand between your crotch and the pommel and one hand between your back and the cantle. A seat that is too small will hurt and adversely influence your elasticity; a saddle that is too large may make you slide.

• With the shortest length of stirrup you are going to use, your knees should not be in front of the knee rolls. With the longest length, the knees should not be too far behind the knee rolls.

• A correct seat provides shoulder, hip, and heel in one vertical line. Check if the stirrup leather is hanging down vertically. If your feet move it forward or back to gain correct position, the stirrup bar is not in the right place. Sitting wrong will greatly influence your leg position, bringing it either too far back or forward.

• When you intend to buy a saddle, you must test if it fits your anatomy. Also a saddle that fits a man perfectly could hurt a woman as the female pelvis is wider than the male's.

• A lot of saddles have different flap lengths. They need to be the right length for your leg. Test with the stirrup leathers you will use. If the flap is too short, the inside upper end of the boot may hook underneath the end of the flap. When the flap is too long, it will be difficult to get through with the pushing leg. So choose the flap lengths that suit your leg length.

THE BRIDLE/AUXILIARY REINS

When introducing the basics of dressage to horse and rider, a snaffle bridle with nose band usually is appropriate and sufficient. Bitless head pieces may be used for short periods when the horse has an injured mouth or teeth. They can also spare the horse aches and pains with a beginner who has extreme difficulty keeping his hands quiet. However, to keep our aids in continuous interaction with the horse, a bridle with bit is essential. During advanced training stages, when collection is established in the horse and the rider has gained an independent and completely controlled seat, the double bridle will be introduced. Stronger-acting bits are not used to have more power over the horse, but intended to influence with more sensitivity.

The snaffle bridle

For basic dressage training we use a snaffle bridle with nose band. The bridle has to be fitted on the horse bringing the cheek pieces up so that the bit is in the tooth-free part of the horse's mouth and high enough that a few little wrinkles show in the corners of the mouth. If too low, this will eventually encourage the horse to bring his tongue above the bit, which leads to less sensitivity on the rein. If too high, this can hurt the mouth and make the horse uncomfortable.

Under normal conditions, the beginner should use single or double-jointed bits of medium thickness at the outside ends. The stronger the bit, the thinner it is. It must be exactly as wide as the horse's mouth.

Riders often switch from one kind of mouth piece to another when training does not proceed as desired or a problem occurs. This may be appropriate at times, but in most cases the rider needs to change what is on the other end of the rein, his hands. A different bit cannot better the rider's feeling in his rein aids and the independence of his seat. Observe some of the big trainers who take time and care to train their horses. Usually they will only work them with a plain snaffle bit.

Nose bands

A proper nose band is part of a dressage bridle. Which one you use depends on the individual horse. Buckled correctly the horse cannot open his mouth to avoid the rein aids. The nose band should only be tightened to where one or two fingers still fit easily underneath. By using a nose band, part of the rein pressure on the bit gets transferred onto the horse's nose. It is very important to fit the nose band properly.

Riders sometimes overly tighten the nose band to keep the mouth closed or the tongue from showing. The horse feels constricted and may even have problems breathing easily. Many horses start fighting the rider's hands because of the tightened nose band.

The dropped nose band

The upper strap has to be about four fingers' width above the nostrils. Fit too low, this nose band will disturb breathing. Experience recommends the dropped nose band for training a horse through the lower dressage levels as it best teaches the horse not to open his jaw to avoid rein aids. It is difficult to fit properly on horses with a short mouth, as either the upper strap will sit too low and affect breathing or the lower strap will sit too high and squeeze the sides of the mouth.

The ordinary nose band

This is probably the most common nose band in the States. Its wider strap is positioned two small fingers' width below the horse's cheekbones. The ordinary nose band gives less control of the horse's jaw and tongue than the dropped nose band. It is the only type of nose band used with a double bridle.

The flash nose band

The flash nose band is an ordinary nose band with a smaller strap attached to it that is buckled low like a dropped nose band. This nose band works well for horses that are sufficiently sensitive and those with a short mouth.

The cross-over/grakle nose band

This nose band has two straps crossing on top of the horse's nose, with buckles on the lower and upper strap. It has about the same influence as the flash nose band. It can be set far from the nostrils and therefore not disturb the horse's breathing.

The double bridle

The double bridle should only be used for more advanced riders and horses because its influence is much stronger than the snaffle. When both horse and rider are secure in at least second level, the double bridle can be introduced. It consists of two bits, a small snaffle bit, and a curb bit with chain. The rider works with two reins in each hand, which alone shows that the rider needs to be advanced.

Other bridles

In addition to those bridles listed above, there are several others, with and without a bit. For certain reasons, the bitless hackamore or side pull can be good for short periods instead of a snaffle bridle. When the horse has an injured mouth or teeth, the horse can still be worked while leaving the mouth area free to heal.

Those bridles put strain on the horse's nose and/or around the complete jaw when pressure is applied on the reins. The hackamore is severe when used incorrectly, whereas the side pull is rather soft. Both bitless bridles usually work well for dressage for short periods. The constant soft rein applied in contact dressage riding may make the horse's nose sore. Often the horse doesn't stay sufficiently sensitive and too much rein pressure needs to be applied. Bitless bridles are often used in Western riding, during which the reins stay loose most of the time.

With a well-trained, sensitive, and obedient horse ridden by a beginner, you may try a side pull for a while. This way the beginner's shaking hands will feel softer to the horse, and his mouth can be kept sensitive. Later you should switch to a mouthpiece.

An excellent exercise is riding single sessions with a side pull once in a while during all training stages. Here we can check if the horse stays on the aids and obedient, which proves the correctness of the rider's influence. If the horse works better with a side pull than with a bit, then either a wrong mouthpiece is being used or the rider needs to improve his hand positioning and rein influence.

Auxiliary Reins

Auxiliary reins help the beginning rider handle a horse or help the more advanced rider explain certain positions and body postures to a horse, mostly a young, mistrained, or extremely difficult horse. They help in special situations and certain training stages. They are not supposed to replace thorough gymnasticizing dressage work with force. Misused, they usually lead to a horse that will not perform properly without them, as he has not been "trained" to do so.

Today there are probably as many variations in the use of auxiliary reins to "make the horse do it right" as there are variations of bits and bridles trying to do the same job — and in as short a time as possible. Who wants to waste time and patience if maybe there is a quicker solution? It is horrifying to observe how many riders torture their horses with little "helpers" like draw reins and the newest strong-bit creation in an effort to make the horse sensitive, reach higher training levels, and be successful. The real solution is making yourself a good enough rider to do the job and take whatever time and patience is needed. Since medieval times, riders have invented and misused reins and bits to replace what they lacked in sense, feeling, and body control.

There are always moments and periods during training in which proper use of auxiliary reins can be essential to progress. Here I will only consider auxiliary reins for the beginning rider. During his training, auxiliary reins are sometimes necessary to help out when the rider still needs to learn. We use the auxiliary reins to keep the horse on the bit, which the rider cannot do yet. Only when the horse keeps his head low and his back supple can the beginner gain feeling for seat and aids.

Side reins

Side reins are used for the beginning rider or for lungeing a horse. A schooling horse going in side reins enables the beginner to sit and handle him. This gives the beginner time to concentrate on himself and therefore make faster progress. Side reins help the horse avoid incorrect body positioning because of incorrect aids from the beginner.

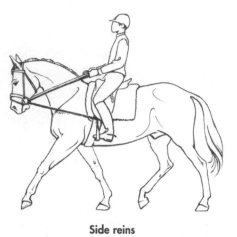

Side reins

The side reins are attached to the girth on both sides of the horse and to the bit rings. Their length is set, so that the horse will not feel them when on the bit properly.

Running martingale

A running martingale is usually used more for jumping or cross-country riding than dressage. A correct fit is important, leaving the martingale long enough that the line of the rein from the horse's mouth to the rider's hand is not interrupted.

The running martingale's main purpose is to prevent the horse from thrusting his head so high that the rider could get hurt. It also makes it easier to keep the horse's head and neck in a steady position.

Personally, I consider the running martingale a perfect step after side reins to encourage the learning rider to get a feel for keeping contact on the reins and riding the horse on the bit. The martingale helps to position the horse's head and neck and mitigates some of the jerks the rider's sometimes shaking hands give. It often has more psychological than actual effect. The horse is restricted only when he moves his head too high. In the correct head and neck position, it does not feel the martingale.

Standing martingale

The standing martingale is similar in make and effect to the running martingale. It is not connected to the reins but attached to the nose band or a small leather strap that is hooked to both bit rings.

Ridden with a standing martingale, the horse may start to contract the lower neck muscle trying to avoid it, making this muscle grow. This is an undesired muscle development.

Draw reins, running reins

Draw reins, or running reins, can be used for lungeing and riding one of two ways. One way is using the draw reins attached to the girth and acting as side reins do. The reins are fastened to the girth between the horse's front legs, lead through the bit rings, and are fastened again on the girth at the horse's sides. In comparison with side reins, the horse can stretch more forward-downward.

The second possibility is that the rider keeps the draw reins coming up through the bit rings in his hands. So the rider uses two pair of reins. The more he shortens the draw reins, the more the horse is forced to lower and shorten his neck. The rider should never use the draw reins more strongly than the normal reins.

As draw reins in a rider's hands give immense power to the rider's rein aids, they must only be used when really necessary and just temporarily. Only advanced riders should use draw reins at all. Draw reins are surely the most misused auxiliary reins.

Chambon, gogue

The chambon and the gogue are mainly used for lungeing the horse. They are excellent to teach a horse to stretch forward-downward and to round and strengthen his back. In addition, the way they act on the horse makes him understand quickly what is wanted.

You should not use them with horses whose head and neck position tends to be too low. The gogue comes with an extra pair of reins to ride with.

About the Author

Ruth Sabine Schaefer lives and works in Frankfurt, Germany. She learned to ride in the classical way and has been an FN licensed trainer since 1984. Schaefer has worked as an instructor and trainer since 1985.

She has trained and competed at all levels in dressage, eventing, and jumping. In earlier years she competed successfully in the Regional Team Eventing championships, Hessen State championships, and German championships.

For several years she managed a stable with a riding school and breeding program. Schaefer has experience teaching riders and horses of all breeds in a variety of disciplines.

Feeling Dressage is her first book.

Photographs by Rob Wilke
Illustrations by Robin Peterson